MANAGING CHA

DIGITAL GOVERNANCE BY DESI

Lisa Welchman

Rosenfeld Media
Brooklyn, New York

Managing Chaos
Digital Governance by Design
By Lisa Welchman

Rosenfeld Media, LLC

457 Third Street, #4R

Brooklyn, New York

11215 USA

On the Web: www.rosenfeldmedia.com

Please send errors to: errata@rosenfeldmedia.com

Publisher: Louis Rosenfeld

Managing Editor: Marta Justak

Interior Layout Tech: Danielle Foster

Cover Design: The Heads of State

Interior Line Art: Michael Tanamachi

Indexer: Sharon Hilgenberg

Proofreader: Kezia Endsley

ISBN: 1-933820-88-8

ISBN-13: 978-1-933820-88-0

LCCN: 2014956861

Printed and bound in the United States of America

This book is dedicated to Rhys—
a good son and a good person.
It's my good luck to be your Mom.

HOW TO USE THIS BOOK

Who Should Read This Book?

Anyone who has an interest and a hand in the strategic management of digital enterprise should read this book, particularly those who serve in bridging and management functions. This includes executive leadership, CIOs, and CMOs, as well as senior domain specialists such as user experience experts, enterprise architects, and content strategists.

People who work at interactive agencies and software integration shops that often have to execute projects amid digital chaos might also find *Managing Chaos* useful reading to help inform their projects and smooth the way for more streamlined project execution.

What's in This Book?

Part I of *Managing Chaos* details a practical methodology for designing and implementing a digital governance framework.

- **Chapter 1** gives a basic definition of digital governance and its core concepts.

- **Chapters 2–5** explore more deeply each of the key aspects of a digital governance framework: digital team structure, digital strategy, digital policy, and digital standards.

- **Chapters 6–8** discuss some of the dynamics around digital governance, including design factors, how to get the design job done, and what to do if your efforts don't get immediate traction in your organization.

Part II of *Managing Chaos* highlights three different governance framework examples: a global multinational company, a government agency, and a higher education-type university. You can use these frameworks to understand some of the practical challenges inherent in designing and implementing your own digital governance framework.

What Comes with This Book?

This book's companion website (🐘rosenfeldmedia.com/books/managing-chaos) contains a blog and additional content. The book's diagrams and other illustrations are available under a Creative Commons license (when possible) for you to download and include in your own presentations. You can find these on Flickr at www.flickr.com/photos/rosenfeldmedia/sets.

FREQUENTLY ASKED QUESTIONS

What is digital governance in the first place?

Digital governance is a discipline that focuses on establishing clear accountability for digital strategy, policy, and standards. A digital governance framework, when effectively designed and implemented, helps to streamline digital development and dampen debates around digital channel "ownership." (See Chapter 1, "The Basics of Digital Governance.")

We don't "govern" things inside our organization. Why should we govern digital?

I don't believe you. Every organization governs something. What you are really saying is that your organization hasn't decided to govern digital. That is one option, but it has consequences. Make sure that you are considering all the possible rationales for not governing digital before you default to this "easy-to-articulate but hard-to-live-with" conclusion. For more, see Chapter 8, "The Decision To Govern Well."

We don't need a governance framework. Can't we just have the main Web team decide everything and run everything? After all, we know what we're doing.

No, that's not a good idea. Creating a digital production silo is not an effective practice. It doesn't allow the digital team to understand the rich landscape of the business. And practically speaking, it's very difficult to size a digital team when all the work is done in one place. For more information on a good digital team structure, see Chapter 2, "Your Digital Team: Where They Are and What They Do."

We're an agile shop, so do we still need governance? Doesn't governance just slow stuff down?

No, governance does the opposite. It enables agility by clarifying roles and responsibilities and connections for a collaborative team. If you think about it, agile software methodology itself is highly structured with well-defined roles and responsibilities. That's why it works so well in the right organizational applications. A digital governance framework, when properly designed, can enable not hinder agile development (see Chapter 1).

OK, I get all the digital governance stuff, and I'm a believer, but I have no authority to establish digital governance in my organization. What do I do if no one cares enough to want to create a framework?

In many ways, this book is just for you. A lot of organizations are led by digitally conservative executives (see Chapter 3, "Digital Strategy: Aligning Expertise and Authority"). Sometimes these conservatives are taking longer than we'd like to wake up to the strategic aspects of digital. While you are waiting for them to pay attention, there are a number of things that you can do to move digital governance efforts forward, including establishing an internal community of practice for digital inside your organization. For more details see Chapter 8.

Aren't policies and standards different ways of talking about the same things? What's the difference between a policy and a standard?

Policies and standards are not the same thing. Policies are organizationally focused high-level statements established to manage risk inside an organization (see Chapter 4, "Staying on Track with Digital Policy"). Standards are focused on establishing development parameters for digital practitioners (see Chapter 5, "Stopping the Infighting About Digital Standards").

Our organization is too innovative for standards. Doesn't creating standards stifle creativity and cutting-edge development?

No, standards can enable innovation and creativity. Standards are the bedrock upon which the Internet and World Wide Web rest. And, we can all agree that there's a lot of innovation and creativity happening on the Internet and Web. Without a framework of digital standards in your organization, yes, you will get some creativity. But, mostly, you will get a chaotic mix of disintegrated content and applications. Having standards and being able to enforce them will allow for rich, creative development (see Chapter 5).

CONTENTS

CHAPTER 10

Government Case Study   181

CHAPTER 11

Higher Education Case Study   197

CODA

FOREWORD

I remember well the day I pitched Cisco's senior staff on leveraging the Web for all our business processes and for creating an organization, job descriptions, and clear roles and responsibilities to support our Web efforts. They agreed, looked around the room, and said, "Which group should do it? (It could have been IT, customer service, or marketing.) Someone said, well, Sinton (marketing), you do it. And that was that. A clear decision, at least in the beginning, and the desktop PC (!) that housed Cisco's website was delivered outside my office along with the person managing it.

And we were off and running—soon envisioning Cisco as a global networked business where the Web improved relationships for all of our business constituents (prospects, customers, investors, suppliers, employees, etc.). It was somewhat easy at first to maintain the "presentation layer" (now called *UX*) and core functions, such as registration databases, content management, and search. We built them from scratch and had a mandate from our CEO to manage them. Cisco's embrace of the Web as a core business strategy was both a strength and a weakness. With so much "embracing," there began turf wars and disintegration that played out, sometimes very clearly, on the customer, employee, and partner websites.

We were developing a new tool for business while working in the fastest growing company of the 1990s. It was chaos, and it became clear that top-down, cross-functional and international coordination was needed to effectively deliver on the promise of the Web. And so we began to experiment with governance models, ultimately landing upon a lead "business council" with supporting cross-functional teams at various levels to help our work be more effective. This business council had at its core an alliance between marketing and IT.

This solved some of our challenges, but not all. Clearly, Cisco was ahead of its time in leveraging the Web for business. In 1996, 20–25% of all Web commerce was done on cisco.com, yet we struggled as we continued to scale, decentralize, and globalize our business. We learned, over time, that it takes the full width and breadth of the organization to support the company's digital efforts, and that it needs to be addressed and coordinated at many levels of the organization from executive to individual contributors.

If only we'd had this book as we blazed that trail, we could have been even more productive and even more customer focused. I'm so thankful that someone as brilliant as Lisa recognized what was happening, both at a tactical and at an organizational development level, and wrote about it. I still believe in the power of the Web to change the way we live, work, play, and learn. Hopefully, Lisa's insights in the area of digital governance will help even more companies unlock that power and potential.

—Chris Sinton
Chair Emeritus StartOut
Co-Founder and Founding President & CEO Network for Good
Internet Trailblazer Cisco Systems

INTRODUCTION

The organizational manifestation of digital governance problems can lead to complicated outcomes like power struggles and other negative competitive behavior in organizations. This is nothing new for organizations, but with the advent of the World Wide Web and Internet, those power struggles now manifest themselves publically and online 24 hours a day, 7 days a week. Many executives and digital leaders assume that this manifestation of chaos is just the state of affairs for digital. But it doesn't have to be this way.

Managing Chaos seeks to address digital governance challenges by offering a practical methodology for calming and clarifying roles and responsibilities of digital development. Digital will never be "simple." The very nature of the digital beast implies complexity—complexity in delivery and complexity in the teams that innovate, develop, and manage digital functionality. With all that complexity, proceeding without some clarity of roles and responsibilities is unlikely to lead to success.

As Vint Cerf, inventor of the Internet said: "Every possible bad thing that can happen in the real world can now happen on the Internet."[1] That means that organizations need to put into place governing principles that maximize the good things that happen and minimize the bad. *Managing Chaos* offers a framework in which that optimization can occur.

---

1 He made this comment at the Internet 2020 meeting sponsored by Duke University School of Law in October 2014.

PART I

Making a Digital Governance Framework

This section contains the fundamentals required to develop a digital governance framework and includes basic definitions, practical guidelines for development, and some of the dynamics that need to be taken into consideration when designing an organizational digital governance framework.

The Basics of Digital Governance

In 1995, when my son was eight months old (Figure 1.1), I packed up my family and moved to Silicon Valley to work with 500 Start-ups' Dave McClure's very first start-up, Aslan Computing. Dave had sent me a 14.4 modem and an HTML book as a baby shower gift, and coding Web pages was a good stay-at-home-mom job. At Aslan, we coded pages for the Netscape website. We invented out-of-the-box website building tools with names like "Ready, Intranet, Go!" We figured out how to manage an ISO 9001 certification process online and built lots of websites for dotcoms, most of which rose and fell quickly in the stew pot of 1990s Silicon Valley.

FIGURE 1.1
Baby Welchman circa 1995.

Late in 1996, I took a job at Cisco Systems, managing the product pages for its website (see Figure 1.2). The site was huge for its time (200K+ HTML pages), and the Web team was relatively small. There was the main site, "Cisco Connection Online," as well as various "country pages." Cisco was getting recognition for being a leader in ecommerce, and folks like Jan Johnston Tyler and Chris Sinton were doing pioneering work in multichannel content delivery. The whole Cisco ship was being steered by John Chambers.

Back then, corporate websites were so new, resources to manage them so few, and Web skills so ill-defined and shallow that people like me who knew only enough HTML and UNIX to be dangerous were let loose on the live production servers of major corporate websites to do whatever we wanted. At Cisco, we invented a lot. We laughed a lot. We accidently erased content a lot. (I remember accidently replacing the Cisco.com homepage with the Japanese Cisco.com homepage once.) The Web team tried almost any idea because there were no rules. The norm was to make it up as you went along. And we did. It was fun, and it couldn't have happened any other way.

FIGURE 1.2

The original Cisco site in 1996.

But, in the years I was at Cisco, I noticed something. Cisco Systems was the epitome of all things Internet and Web. It wasn't just that it sold routers, hubs, and switches. It wasn't just that Cisco installed a high-speed Internet connection in its employees' homes. Cisco as a company was serious about using the Web as a business tool. In 1996, Cisco had all its technical documentation online, downloadable software images, a robust intranet, and a rapidly growing B-to-B ecommerce model. But, despite all of this cutting-edge use of the

World Wide Web, Cisco still had a lot of problems managing its own website.

There were internal debates over homepage real estate by various business units. There was an ever-present debate about who (the marketing team or the technology team) ought to be selecting and implementing key website technologies like search engine software and other, then newer, technologies such as Web content management systems and portal software. At almost every meeting about the website, more than half the time was spent not actually determining what type of functionality needed to be implemented, but on who got to *decide* what functionality would be implemented.

Competing factions would show up at meetings with different website designs, information architectures, and technologies, and the debate would go on and on. People would get angry. Managers would fight. Office politics raged. But after all the drama, the solution usually ended up being that *no* decisions were made. We left the room only to come back for rounds two, three, and four once tempers had cooled off. What that meant in practical terms was that often multiple competing technologies were deployed and multiple website designs implemented—each area implementing its own vision over the part of the site that it "owned." The result was a graphically diverse, incongruent website with a confused information architecture.

And I was part of the problem. I was part of the marketing team that felt that we owned the whole site—because websites are communications vehicles first and foremost, right? The evil nemesis on the other side of our debates was usually the IT team, who was constantly pointing out that the website was first and foremost a technology. I wasn't thinking about governance per se back then. But, being tasked with leading the team to select the first content management system for Cisco Connection Online, I was frequently caught straddling the line between marketing and technology. I was beginning to see that both teams had valuable contributions to make, not only in the selection process but also in the overall running of the site. Still the battles raged on.

Eventually, the cross-departmental content-management product-selection team we had assembled narrowed our candidates down to a single vendor. All the stakeholders (marketing, IT, hands-on Web folks, managers, and senior managers) assembled in a conference room. We'd written a requirements document, installed and tested the software for months over a number of use cases, negotiated pricing, and pretty much driven the vendor crazy. It was time to make the decision. Both the vendor's implementation team and the software had passed all of our tests and the price was right, but still the people around the table were reluctant to make the commitment to buy the software.

There we were: the right people around the table, the right solution in front of us, and we still couldn't make a decision. That's when I began to understand what was really going on. It wasn't that we couldn't make a decision because we weren't sure about what the right solution was; we couldn't make a decision because no one really knew whose job it was to say "yes" or "no." I also began to realize that the uncertainty didn't stop at CMS software selection, because no one knew whose job it was to decide *anything* about the website: content, design, information architecture, applications, and on and on. And, without that clarity about decision-making, the extended digital team at Cisco could argue about the website pretty much in perpetuity.

The Cisco Web team had a governance problem.

In a moment I'm still proud of, I stepped forward and broke the stalemate by assuming the authority that had never been formally placed. I said, "Let's do it. We'll be at greater risk continuing to manage our content the way we do now than if we implement this CMS." Thus, we moved forward.

I liked that feeling of breaking stalemates and helping Web teams move forward, and I wanted to spend more time with my four-year-old son. So I left Cisco in 1999 to become a consultant. By then, the scope of Cisco Connection was off the charts (over 10M Web pages, 200,000 registered website users, and 400 content developers worldwide). I figured if Cisco with all its Web smarts found it hard to manage its website and Web team, other companies with the same problems probably would need help as well.

They did.

Fast-forward to today. My son is in university (see Figure 1.3), and on a typical day, I pick up the phone, and it's a call from an organization that is having trouble managing its Web presence. Maybe it's a large, global company with over 200 websites in many different languages. Or maybe they aren't really sure how many sites they have or who is managing them. Perhaps their main site was hacked several times last year, and some of their customer personal information has been compromised. Maybe it's a national government trying to figure out how to govern its national Web presence. Or it could be a university with a lot of headstrong PhDs who want to do their own thing online and a student body that expects an integrated user experience from their university.

FIGURE 1.3
It's 18 years later, and he's on his way to university.

Usually, our conversation starts with the clients telling me how they're going to solve their problems. I hear the same solutions all the time. Most digital and Web managers try to design their way out of a low-quality, high-risk digital presence with a website graphical interface redesign, a new information architecture, a technology re-platform, or a content strategy—and everything will be better. Often, it is better for a few months or a few quarters, and then the digital system begins to degrade again. Maybe a few rogue websites have popped up, or the core digital team finds out that there are a bunch of poorly implemented social accounts. This scenario happens over and over again because organizations haven't addressed the underlying governance issues for their digital presence.

Along with fixing websites or applications and strategizing about content, organizations need to undertake a design effort to determine the most effective way to make decisions and work together to sustain their digital face. They need a digital governance framework. But, often, when I tell organizations that (another) redesign or CMS probably isn't going to fix their problem and that they need to take the time to address their governance concerns, I often get all kinds of pushback:

"We work in silos. That's our culture. We don't *govern* anything!"

"We need to be agile and innovative. Governance just slows things down."

"We don't have time to design a digital governance framework. We've got too many *real* problems with our website."

In the face of a 15- or 20-year-old technically incongruent, content-bloated, low-quality website, here's my challenge:

- Isn't it better to take the time to come up with some basic rules of engagement for digital than to deal day-in and day-out with unresolved debates over content site "ownership," graphics, social media moderation, and the maintenance websites?

- How many lawsuits, how many security breeches, and how many customers and employees do you have to annoy before you realize that governing your digital presence makes sense?

- What's the bare minimum that needs to be controlled about your digital presence in order to manage risk, raise quality, and still allow different aspects of the organization the flexibility they need?

Isn't governance the better choice?

Why "Governance?"

I'm often asked if I can find a more user-friendly word than "governance."

No, I can't.

For many, the word "governance" conjures up an image of an organizational strait jacket. Governance to them means forcing people to work in a small box or making everyone work the same way. They'd rather have me use words like "team building" or "collaboration model." I usually refuse. Governance is good. And, after reading *Managing Chaos* and applying its guidance to your own organization, I hope you'll agree. Governing doesn't have to make business processes bureaucratic and ineffective. In fact, I'd argue that "bureaucratic and ineffective" describe how digital development works in your organizations right now—with no governance.

Governance is an enabler. It allows organizations to minimize some of the churn and uncertainty in development by clearly establishing accountability and decision-making authority for all matters digital. That doesn't mean that the people who aren't decision makers can't provide input or offer new and innovative ideas. Rather, it means that at the end of the day, after all the information is considered, the organization clearly understands how decisions will be made about the digital portfolio.

There are many different ways to govern an organization's digital presence effectively. Your job is to discover the way that works best for your digital team. Your digital governance framework should enable a dynamic that allows your organization to get its digital business done effectively—whether you're a bleeding-edge online powerhouse or a global B-to-B with a bunch of slim "business card" websites. A good digital governance framework will establish a sort of digital development DNA that ensures that your digital presence evolves in a manner that is in harmony with your organization's strategic objectives. A digital governance framework isn't bureaucratic and ineffective. Properly designed, a digital governance framework can make your online business machine sing.

The proof is out there. Wikipedia is, arguably, one of the most substantively and collaboratively governed websites on the Web, but it is also perceived as a site that fosters a high degree of freedom of expression. The well-defined open standards of the World Wide Web Consortium (W3C) enable the World Wide Web to exist, as it is—without which we would not even be having this conversation. And the multiplicity of purpose and diversity apparent on the World Wide Web speaks for itself.

Your organization needs its own internal W3C, so to speak, so that departments, schools, lines of business—however you segment your organization—can be free to take advantage of digital channels, but within parameters that make sense for the organization's mission, goals, and bottom line. In addition, it needs to intentionally design its digital team so that it can work efficiently and productively. And that's the work of a digital governance framework.

This is your chance to establish the foundational framework that will influence the direction of digital in your organization for years to come. Business leaders and senior digital leaders need to get together and establish how to govern and manage digital effectively in their organizations. Now. Through *Managing Chaos*, you will learn how to free your organization from debate-stalled stagnation around digital development and establish an environment where an entire organization can work together to successfully leverage all that digital has to offer.

What Is Digital Governance?

Digital governance is a framework for establishing accountability, roles, and decision-making authority for an organization's digital presence—which means its websites, mobile sites, social channels, and any other Internet and Web-enabled products and services. Having a well-designed digital governance framework minimizes the number of tactical debates regarding the nature and management of an organization's digital presence by making clear who on your digital team has decision-making authority for these areas:

- **Digital strategy:** Who determines the direction for digital?

- **Digital policy:** Who specifies what your organization must and must not do online?

- **Digital standards:** Who decides the nature of your digital portfolio?

When these questions are answered and your digital governance framework is well implemented by leadership, your organization can look forward to a more productive work environment for all digital stakeholders and a higher-quality, more effective digital presence.

The work of the framework is to clarify *who* the decision makers are, but in order to understand who should decide matters related to strategy, policy, and standards, it's important first to understand *what* these things are.

Digital Strategy

A digital strategy articulates an organization's approach to leveraging the capabilities of the Internet and the World Wide Web. A digital strategy has two facets: guiding principles and performance objectives.

- Guiding principles provide stakeholders with a streamlined, qualitative expression of your organization's high-level digital business intent and values.

- Performance objectives quantitatively define what digital success means for an organization.

If your digital strategy is off target, then supporting policy, standards, and the process-related tactical machinations of your digital team will likely be off target as well. So when you are identifying who should establish digital strategy for your organization, it is especially important to include the right set of resources. That set should include the following:

- People who know how to analyze and evaluate the impact of digital in your marketspace.

- People who have the knowledge and ability to conceive an informed and visionary response to that impact.

- People who have the business expertise and authority to ensure that the digital vision is effectively implemented.

In most organizations, your digital strategy team will need to be a mix of executives and senior managers, business analysts, and your most senior digital experts. Luckily, identifying those resources is relatively easy. In fact, right now you could probably sit down and write down your "dream team" for establishing digital strategy. But that's only half of the challenge. Often, the real digital strategy challenge is getting those resources to communicate and work together. The skill sets, experience, work styles, and business language of these two constituents can be very different, and the managerial distance between executives who mandate organizational change and digital experts who implement it can be great. In Chapter 3, "Digital Strategy: Aligning Expertise and Authority," I will focus not only on selecting the right players for establishing digital strategy, but also on how to get that team aligned.

DO'S AND DON'TS

DO: Ensure that your digital strategy takes into account business considerations, as well as your organization's culture toward digital. Not every organization needs to be a ground-breaking, digital go-getter.

Digital Policy

Digital policies are guidance statements put into place to manage risk and ensure that an organization's core interests are served as it operates online. Think of policies as guardrails that keep the organization's digital presence from going off the road.

The substance of digital policy should influence the behavior of employees when they are developing material for online channels. For example, the policy might specify that developers should not build applications that collect email addresses of children, because the company doesn't want to violate their organization's online privacy policy regarding children. Or perhaps content developers at a pharmaceutical company might be made aware of the differences in national policy as it relates to talking about the efficacy of their products online.

Because digital policy is a subset of corporate policy, it naturally inherits the corporate policy's broad scope and diversity. Due to this scope and diversity, typically, a single individual or group *cannot* effectively author policy. This approach sometimes comes as a surprise to digital teams who feel that policy authorship falls naturally into their camp. That scenario occurs because organizations often conflate policy and standards; however, the two areas are not the same. Policies exist to protect the organization. They do not address online quality and how to achieve it—*that* is the role of standards.

A digital governance framework ought to designate a policy steward who is accountable for ensuring that all digital policy issues are addressed. Digital policy steward(s) should have a relatively objective, informed, and comprehensive view of the implications of digital for the organization. Digital policy authors are a diverse set of organizational resources who can contribute to and shape an appropriate organizational position for a given policy topic. In Chapter 4 "Staying on Track with Digital Policy," I'll go into more detail about the responsibilities of the policy steward and offer suggestions for which person or people ought to be authoring policy within organizations.

DO'S AND DON'TS

DON'T: Forget that digital policy is a subset of corporate policy and needs to be in harmony with other policies within your organization. For instance, digital policy is often informed by fiscal policy, IT policy, or vertical, market-focused external policy.

Wikipedia is a free encyclopedia, which is written by the people who use it in many different languages, as you can see in Figure 1.4.

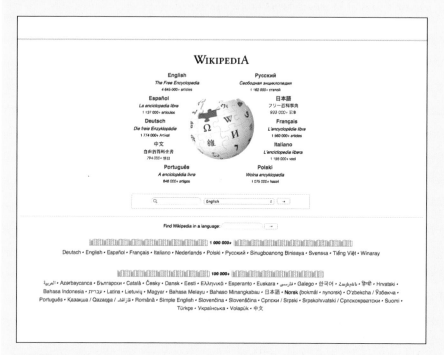

FIGURE 1.4

Wikipedia: an encyclopedia for the world.

The "Five Pillars" of Wikipedia (an online free encyclopedia) represent a great example of how to design guiding principles for an organization. These pillars/principles capture the culture, values, and goals of the organization as it relates to the Wikipedia digital properties, and they provide clear directions to the Wikipedia development community. They are as follows:

Wikipedia is an encyclopedia.

It combines many features of general and specialized encyclopedias, almanacs, and gazetteers. Wikipedia is not a soapbox, an advertising platform, a vanity press, an experiment in anarchy or democracy, an indiscriminate collection of information, or a Web directory. It is not a dictionary, a newspaper, or a collection of source documents, although some of its fellow Wikimedia projects are.

Wikipedia is written from a neutral point of view.

We strive for articles that document and explain the major points of view, giving due weight with respect to their prominence in an impartial tone. We avoid advocacy, and we characterize information and issues rather than debate them. In some areas, there may be just one well-recognized point of view; in others, we describe multiple points of view, presenting each accurately and in context rather than as "the truth" or "the best view." All articles must strive for verifiable accuracy, citing reliable, authoritative sources, especially when the topic is controversial or a living person. Editors' personal experiences, interpretations, or opinions do not belong.

Wikipedia is free content that anyone can edit, use, modify, and distribute.

Since all editors freely license their work to the public, no editor owns an article, and any contributions can and will be mercilessly edited and redistributed. Respect copyright laws, and never plagiarize from sources. Borrowing non-free media is sometimes allowed as fair use, but strive to find free alternatives first.

Editors should treat each other with respect and civility.

Respect your fellow Wikipedians, even when you disagree. Apply Wikipedia etiquette and avoid personal attacks. Seek consensus, avoid edit wars, and never disrupt Wikipedia to illustrate a point. Act in good faith and assume good faith on the part of others. Be open and welcoming to newcomers. If a conflict arises, discuss it calmly on the nearest talk pages, follow dispute resolution, and remember that there are 4,261,587 articles on the English Wikipedia to work on and discuss.

Wikipedia does not have firm rules.

Wikipedia has policies and guidelines, but they are not carved in stone; their content and interpretation can evolve over time. Their principles and spirit matter more than their literal wording, and sometimes improving Wikipedia requires making an exception. Be bold, but not reckless, in updating articles, and do not agonize about making mistakes. Every past version of a page is saved, so any mistakes can be easily corrected.

---

1 http://en.wikipedia.org/wiki/Wikipedia:Five_pillars

Table 1.1 outlines the basic areas for policy consideration. Some organizations will need to address a more comprehensive set of policies based on their objectives or digital audience. For instance, organizations that support a digital presence for young children may have a specific children's online privacy policy, or those people in healthcare may have to directly address patient and medical information that is related to privacy concerns. In fact, sometimes policies might have to be drafted to address constraints related to particular geographic regions such as states, nations, and unions.

TABLE 1.1 A LIST OF BASIC DIGITAL POLICY

Policy Topic	Description
Accessibility	Details the accessibility level that must be followed to ensure that all users can interact with your organization online.
Branding	Determines how your organization maintains its desired identity while online.
Domain Names	Manages the purchase, registration, and use of Internet domain names.
Language and Localization	Establishes parameters for language used in conducting business online and special information related to making content appropriate for locales globally. These include translation, idiom usage, imagery, and so on.
Hyperlinks and Hyperlinking	Determines how and when it is appropriate and inappropriate to hyperlink to content on the World Wide Web within and external to the organization.
Intellectual Property	Covers copyright and other ownership for information gathered, delivered, and used online.
Privacy	Covers the privacy needs of employees and users when interacting with the organization online. Specific technologies that are unique to the Web (like "cookies" and other tracking devices) are defined and their use discussed.
Security	Defines measures that will be taken to ensure that information delivered online (and used in transactions) and provided by customers and employees is used in the manner intended and not intercepted, monitored, used, or distributed by parties not intended.
Social Media	Addresses parameters for the use of social software within the organization.
Web Records Management	Specifies the full lifecycle management of content delivered and generated on the World Wide Web. May also include the disposition of transactional log files.

Digital Standards

Standards articulate the exact nature of an organization's digital portfolio. They exist to ensure optimal digital quality and effectiveness. Standards are both broad and deep. They address a broad range of topics with depth, such as overall user experience and content strategy concerns, as well as tactical specifications related to issues like a website's component-based content model or replicable code snippets. That's a lot of territory to cover. So, usually, it will take an equally broad and deep range of resources to contribute to and define digital standards.

Often, when I am brought in to resolve organizational governance concerns, the root of the problem is a disagreement about who gets to define those standards. Sometimes, the disagreement can be quite contentious with various righteous digital stakeholders coming to the debate armed with expertise (Web team), platform ownership (IT), and budget and mission (business units and departments)—all equally sure that they should be the final decision-maker.

A digital governance framework gives each of these stakeholder types an appropriate role to play in the definition of standards. In Chapter 5, "Stopping the Infighting About Digital Standards," I'll explore in detail how to assign stewardship and authorship to standards. When these roles are assigned, time-consuming debates about functionality will be minimized and an environment of collaboration for a better digital quality and effectiveness will emerge.

DO'S AND DON'TS

DO: Make sure that you document the full range of digital standards, which includes design, editorial, publishing and development, and network and server standards. Often, digital workers just focus on editorial and design standards and neglect the other categories.

The Power of the Framework

A digital governance framework is a system that delegates authority for digital decision-making about particular digital products and services from the organizational core to other aspects of the organization, as shown in Figure 1.5. Digital governance frameworks have less to do with who in your organization performs the hands-on work of digital and more to do with who has the authority to decide the nature of your websites, mobile apps, and social channels. That means a digital governance framework does *not* specify a production process. It does *not* articulate a content strategy, information architecture, or whether or not you work in an agile or waterfall development environment. What a digital governance framework *does* is specify who has the authority to make those decisions. This explicit separation of production processes from decision-making authority for standards is what gives the framework its power.

If you consider your own situation, it's likely that most organizational debates about digital are not about who does the work, but rather about the way your websites look or what digital functionality should or should not be built and how those efforts are funded. In my experience, most digital stakeholders are so disinterested in doing the day-to-day grunt work of digital that a relatively small, central digital team is completely overburdened by tactical development tasks, while an army of digital stakeholders (who want to put little or no resources, fiscal or human, and effort into ensuring the work gets done) use their organizational authority to dictate how websites should look, which applications should be developed, and which social channels ought to be supported. This unbalanced situation leads to a contentious, resentful work environment, and more importantly, to a low-quality, ineffective digital product. The overburdened digital team stays in this situation because doing all the work is often the only way they can ensure that best practices and their standards are adhered to—because there is no governance framework, and the only way they can ensure standards compliance is by doing all the work themselves.

Having a digital governance framework brings digital development back into balance by separating day-to-day digital production functions and decision making for strategy, policy, and standards. For a long time, daily Web page maintenance and responsibility for the look-and-feel and functionality of websites has been concentrated in the hands of a few people in the organization. Perhaps this strategy

Your Organization Scope: *What are you governing?*	Core						
Digital Governance Sponsorship and Advocacy							
DIGITAL STRATEGY							
Digital Strategy Definition							
DIGITAL POLICY							
Policy Stewardship							
Policy Authoring							
DIGITAL STANDARDS							
Standards Stewardship							
Design Standards Definition							
Editorial Standards Definition							
Publishing & Development Standards Definition							
Network & Infrastructure Standards Definition							

FIGURE 1.5

The digital governance framework accountability grid.

was effective in the early days of digital production. But, today, with a more complex digital presence that includes not just websites but also mobile and social software interactions, digital production needs to be distributed throughout the organization. In order for production decentralization to be done effectively, a strategy and policies and standards need to be clearly communicated so that all people working with digital know what to do and what not to do. A digital governance framework provides that clarity.

When this effective decentralization of production happens, two important things occur:

Dispersed Core				Distributed			Ad Hoc	Extended							

- The workload and expense of digital developing is shared throughout the organization.

- The organization can leverage the knowledge assets of their entire organization to inform and support its digital portfolio.

And that's really powerful.

DO'S AND DON'TS

DO: Understand where you are on the digital maturity curve before you start your framework design effort. Most organizations can't make the leap from chaotic digital development environment to a responsive one in a single bound!

The Range of Digital Standards

When you establish decision-making authority for standards, you will discover that it takes collaboration among resources with a broad range of competencies in order to create an effective set of standards that work together (see Table 1.2).

TABLE 1.2   DIGITAL STANDARDS CATEGORIES

Standards Domain	Influence Over
Design The graphical presentation layer of digital.	Interactive (video design, podcasts, forms, applications) Typography and Color (symbols, bullets, lists, fonts typeface and size, color palette) Templates (page components, pop-up windows, tables, email) Images (background images, photos, buttons, and icons)
Editorial The style of language and the strategy for content delivery and curation.	Branding (tone, use of company name, use of product names) Language (style manual/dictionary, terminology, cultural competence) Localization (translation, management, cultural adaptation)
Publishing and Development Information management, development protocols, and publishing and infrastructure tools that impact the architectural aspects of information organization and delivery.	Information Organization and Access (information architecture, taxonomy, metadata, file-naming conventions, Web records management, accessibility) Tools (portal, Web content management, search, translation management, document management, collaboration, digital asset management, surveying, webcasts, social software, Web analytics, usability) Development Protocols (RSS links and specifications, multimedia, operating systems, browser compatibility, browser detection, load time, single sign-on, mobile, password management, FTP, frames, personal data collection, code, file types, cookies and sign-in, personal data retention , non-HTML content)

TABLE 1.2 continued

Standards Domain	Influence Over
Network and Server The platform-focused aspects of digital production.	**Domains** (domain format/names, use of domain name, domain name redirects, vanity/marketing domains) **Hosting** (site backup, disaster recovery, supported connection speed, personal data retention) **Security** (personally identifiable information, ebusiness/financial transactions, security protocols to protect information, visitor data and traceability, firewall rules, data safety and transmission intrusion detection, alerting mechanism, monitoring mechanism SSL, passwords, time-outs and auto log-offs) **Server Software** (databases, DB naming conventions, app server, Web server, virtual private network [VPN], operating system, domain name server, load balancer, file server, maintaining licensing keys, single sign-on, server analytics, wireless application protocol [WAP], maintaining warranties and servicing) **Server Hardware** (standard Web server configuration, database, app server, Web server, firewall appliance, maintaining warranties and servicing, test servers, caching)

Your Digital Governance: How Bad Is It?

Rest assured—every organization has digital governance problems. Just because an organization might look good online doesn't mean that it is getting a good return on its investment or operating in an effective, low-risk environment. I've seen plenty of "lipstick-on-pig" digital environments where a nice-looking website design was only thinly veiling an ineffective digital presence supported by no real digital strategy and an uncoordinated digital team—governance gone wild! I've also seen some "looks like it was built in 1997" websites where the site was getting real work done for the organization, and the supporting organization was only inches away from governing well. Looks can be deceiving.

How can you tell how well your organization is doing? Instead of looking at your (and your competitor's) websites, social channels, and mobile apps to judge how well you are governing, you can understand where you are on the digital governance maturity curve (see Table 1.3).

You'll probably find that your organization is at different levels of maturity for different aspects of the framework (team structure, digital strategy, digital policy, and digital standards). That's normal. Maybe you work in a heavily regulated industry, and you're "mature" when it comes to digital policy, but you lack standards. Or maybe you have some policy and standards, but you have no real digital strategy. The point is for you to assign responsibility and accountability to the right set of resources so that the substance of your strategy, policies, and standards is on target, laying the foundation for your digital team to create real online value for the organization.

Once you've finished designing your framework, you will find that accountability and authority for strategy, policy, and standards will be distributed throughout your organization's digital team. But do you know who your digital team is and what they do? Maybe not. So before we examine how to determine accountability for each of the digital governance components, let's take a look at how digital teams are structured. Just as websites grow organically and without much of a plan, so do digital teams. It's important to take the time to establish and put into place a well-defined digital team before you begin your governance design efforts.

Understanding Digital Governance Maturity

There is a digital governance maturity curve (see Figure 1.6) that most organizations move through when they launch a digital channel (Web, mobile, or social). The process of maturity begins with the decision to launch a new channel, and it culminates with the organization having fully integrated that channel into the company to the extent that governing dynamics and operational processes are automatic, leaving the organization fully responsive to digital trends.

The dynamics of each phase are fairly distinct. Most organizations that are seeking to improve digital governance are usually in the "chaos" phase, while some are stalled at "basic management" and trying to move to the next level. Also, organizations are typically at different places on this curve, depending on which digital channel is being considered. For example, an organization might be at "basic management" for websites, but at "launch" for its mobile channel, while in "chaos" for social channels. This issue can add complexity when designing a digital governance framework.

FIGURE 1.6

The digital governance maturity curve.

GOVERNANCE AND DIGITAL ANALYTICS

Phil Kemelor, EY

In my work with Fortune 500 companies, government agencies, and national non-profit organizations, the linkage between smart Web governance and intelligent use of analytics data goes hand-in-hand. Governance sets the tone for a culture of analytics through clear definition of strategy and direction as to what metrics and measurement guide accountability in achieving goals related to the strategy.

Maturity Stage	Dynamics
Launch	Research and development mode, as the digital functionality or channel is being informally tested or formally piloted.
	Basic policy constraints are considered to ensure that the organization is operating within the bounds of the law and any other regulatory constraints.
	There are few standards imposed at this point because the organization is just going to "try out" new functionality to see if there is value to the organization.
Organic Growth	Aspects of functionality "work." Others in the organization begin to leverage the work of the piloting team.
	Functional and systemic redundancy begins (design, technology, process).
	Some progressive executives may understand the value of the channel, but deep value and mature business measurement tactics are not being applied.
	Functionality is thought of as a "cost center," not a core revenue generator.
	Basic policy constraints are still in place, and some may be documented.
	There are usually few standards in place. Considerations around basic corporate standards, such as branding, begin to arise.
Chaos	Executives and senior management are aware of the digital channel, but they have likely wholly delegated the creation of digital strategy to junior resources.
	Different organizational departments have created organizationally incongruent digital strategies. Competition for "ownership" begins to emerge.
	The organization is unable to identify and account for all its digital assets or the people who execute on and fund digital development inside the organization.
	Core marketing communications and IT policy are beginning to be formalized—sometimes separate from the stewardship and influence of the corporate legal team.
	Some standards are documented, but many core digital standards are missing.

TABLE 1.3 continued

Maturity Stage	Dynamics
Basic Management	Executives and senior digital experts have begun a dialogue regarding the strategy for digital.
	The organization begins to consider its digital budget.
	Digital quality measurement tactics, systems, and software are emplaced.
	Some design, functionality, and platform normalization has begun, and efforts are made to reduce redundancies where they exist and where it is effective.
	A core digital center of excellence is beginning to emerge, although it may not have all of the desired authority.
	Performance is evaluated by examining tactical analytics like website "page hits" and number of "likes" in social media channels.
	The existence of a set of digital policies and standards is in place.
	Basic cross-organization collaboration teams begin to appear, such as "Web Councils" and standards development teams.
Responsive	"Digital" is fully integrated within the organization and is no longer a functional silo.
	The digital team is clearly identified, organized, and funded.
	Accountability for digital strategy is clearly placed.
	A guiding principle for digital development is established.
	Performance indicators are defined, and mechanisms and programs for quality and success measurements are in place.
	Digital policy stewards and policy authors are identified.
	The process for external and internal policy review is in place.
	Digital standards steward(s) and authors are identified, and standards compliance and measurement mechanisms are implemented.

Summary

- Digital governance is a framework for establishing accountability, roles, and decision-making authority for an organization's digital presence. It addresses three topics: strategy, policy, and standards.

- Digital strategy articulates the organization's approach to leveraging the capabilities of the Internet and World Wide Web. It is authored by those who can evaluate the impact of digital on your marketspace and come up with an effective strategy for success.

- Digital policies are guidance statements put into place to manage the organizational risk inherent with operating online. They should be informed by digital, organizational, and legal experts.

- Digital standards are guidance statements for developing the organizational digital presence. They should be informed and defined by subject matter experts.

- A digital governance framework delegates authority for digital decision-making about particular digital products and services from the organizational core to other aspects of the organization. This allows the organization to effectively decentralize production maintenance of its digital presence.

CHAPTER 2

Your Digital Team: Where They Are and What They Do

I'm a real fan of music—any kind of music, as long as it's got some soul to it to. But, if I had to play favorites, I'd have to say that I like symphony orchestras and small jazz ensembles the most. In my mind, they represent two ends of the musical spectrum—like the yin and yang of music. Jazz seems on the surface to be highly unstructured and free. Alternately, orchestral music has a reputation for being really prescribed and controlled. But it's not that simple. Embedded in each of these styles of music is its inverse—so, orchestral music at its best can be wildly evocative and free, and improvisational jazz, that sounds so unformed, usually operates over a mathematical grid of tonality. Thus, the symphony has the emotional richness we associate easily with jazz music, and within jazz lies the discipline we associate with orchestral music, as shown in Figure 2.1.

FIGURE 2.1
The Baltimore Symphony Orchestra and Time for Three perform at Carnegie Hall's *Spring for Music* festival.

SOURCE: http://rfld.me/1SOYKHg

But, if you look at the interactions and artifacts required for a typical hour's worth of quality jazz versus an hour's worth of quality orchestral music, you'll see a big difference. Jazz musicians *might* have a few lead sheets, which detail the melody of a tune and its basic harmonic framework, whereas the orchestral conductor is faced with a relatively thick score, usually marked up with further notes and cues. Jazz musicians might have a 10-minute conversation before they start their gig, but a symphony orchestra may spend an afternoon or more starting and stopping a piece, paying close attention to the tricky parts where the group might stumble over each other. And, even before the orchestra musicians get together to rehearse, various orchestral sections may get together to work through concerns related to their section, like bowing strategies for string players. It's not an accident that all the bows in a violin section all move together!

In the end, both the jazz trio and the orchestra can deliver a powerful performance that satisfies the audience. And both groups rely on the competence and expertise of individual musicians. The difference lies in the fact that one group makes it up as they go along and sees where it takes them, while the other one doesn't. It's a different means to an end and that means is dictated by one thing primarily—the size of the group involved. It's easier to get three or four people to collaborate and invent in real time than it is to get 100 people to do so.

It's likely that your organization's early Web team was like a jazz trio—that is, a group of highly engaged people with special skills working on one website and making things up as they went along. And it worked—for a while. Now, 15 or 20 years later, an organization might have 10, 100, or 500 people and an array of external support vendors putting in effort to support their digital presence. And, instead of websites being an interesting business oddity, they have become mission critical. Only the problem is that no one has taken the time to mature and intentionally form the digital team that supports those sites—to identify who all those resources are, where they are in the organization, what they are supposed to be doing, and how the whole team should work together as a unit. Just as there are a lot of different ensemble configurations between the small intimacy of the jazz ensemble and the top-down, highly structured orchestra, there are many different types of digital team configurations. Your job is to discover which configuration will work best for your organization so that you have an appropriate canvas upon which to execute your digital governance design work

The real work of a digital governance framework is to assign appropriate authority for digital strategy, policy, and standards decision-making to the right resources within your digital team. But, if you have no sense of where your team members are or what they do, it is almost impossible to assign digital governance authority properly. Let's take a look at your digital team

What Is Your Digital Team?

Your digital team is the full set of resources required to keep the digital process functioning for your organization. Your digital team includes not just the core product-focused teams found in marketing/

communications and IT, but also the casual content contributors, business unit Web managers, supporting software vendors, and organizational agencies of record. Your digital team also includes those who administer and support digital efforts by tending to the programmatic aspects of the digital team, such as budget digital team resource development and management.

DO'S AND DON'TS

> **DON'T:** Worry too much about whether your core digital team is in marketing, communications, or IT (or anywhere else in your organization). Clearly defined roles and authority are much more important than the organizational placement of your core team.

Unfortunately, many organizations identify their digital teams as only the hands-on resources that design, write, and post Web content and create applications on a daily basis. This narrow view of the digital team reinforces the idea that digital is a tactical function and not a strategic one that requires planning and resource management. It also minimizes the deep information and technical architectural issues that must be addressed in order to do digital well and safely for your organization and your users. With a broader perspective of your digital team, it becomes clear that your team is all over your organization, and there comes the realization that there is a diversity of skills required to support digital. Some of those skills existed in your organization prior to digital, and some of the skills are new. Some skills are specifically related to digital expertise, and some of them are related to other domains.

An easy way to get a handle on your digital team is to consider the following (see Figure 2.2):

- The location, role, and budgeting source of your core digital team.

- The location, roles, and budgeting source for your distributed digital team, which can include departmental Web managers, country Web managers, product-focused content contributors, and other satellite teams.

- The authority, role, and budgeting source of any digital steering committees, councils, and working groups.

- The identity of and budgeting source for your extended digital team, which includes agencies of record, software integrators, and other external vendor support.

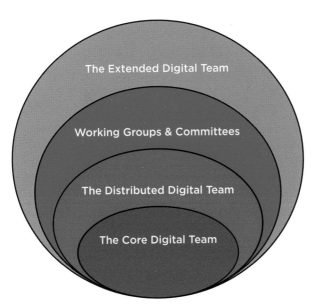

FIGURE 2.2
Components of your
digital team.

Once these aspects are clearly understood, you will have established
a clear resource field upon which to place decision-making authority.
Now, let's look at each aspect of your team in more depth.

Your Core Team

The core digital team's job is to conceptualize, architect, and oversee
the *full* organizational digital presence. In most organizations, the core
digital team is the set of resources you most likely called the "Web
team." In an environment where digital governance is immature, this
team often has de facto authority over digital standards—that is, until
a powerful stakeholder disagrees with them. Often, they are in either
marketing/communications or your IT department. But technically

speaking, the team can be anywhere in the organization. The core team has many responsibilities that can be distilled into two functions: program management and product management.

Core Team Program Management

NOTE PROGRAM MANAGEMENT RESPONSIBILITIES

- Oversees local and global digital staff and budget.
- Implements digital strategy.
- Measures and reports on the effectiveness of digital initiatives
- Informs and authors digital policy.
- Builds and sustains internal digital community of practice.

Program management is the administrative side of digital. Its function is to enable the digital process by ensuring that the digital team is properly resourced, which includes the management of staff, vendors, and capital expenditures. The program management function also oversees the tactical evaluation of the digital team and digital platform performance, in essence measuring how effectively they have implemented the organization's digital strategy.

Core digital team program management resources are an important and often missing link between hands-on digital workers and the rest of the organization. Program management resources offer jargon-free, quantitative and qualitative evidence to leadership in order to garner fiscal and strategic support for the growing resource needs of the digital team. Unfortunately, many organizations have a weak digital program management function. For some, tactics for the measurement of digital performance are elementary with a focus on website page hits and social media "likes" instead of on things like related fiscal business performance and user experience metrics. Usually, no one in the organization has a clear understanding of what is being invested in digital. Often, digital efforts are sustained by the non-strategic leaching of human and fiscal resources from communications and IT budgets. A result of that is an often siloed approach to digital development. In many organizations, resources can be found for initiatives that center on communications or IT-focused tasks like content creation, visual identity, and systems platforms and application development, but the more obscure but essential digital functions like taxonomy, component content modeling, user experience, and digital analytics development are left without support. A mature approach to program management would address the full scope of digital and ensure that staffing and budgeting are adequate for all areas.

Ideally, an organization's core digital program management function would be staffed by individuals who have a firm understanding of the capacity and capabilities of digital and who also have management expertise. In many organizations, the program management function is filled by the Chief Marketing Officer or a senior marketing manager. In organizations that have a stand-alone digital team with communications, digital, and IT resources, this role could be filled by a director or vice president of digital. Or, if much of the core team function resides in the IT department, this program management function could rest with the office of the CIO or some other senior IT manager.

DO'S AND DON'TS

DO: Consider the make-up of your entire digital team. That includes not just hands-on resources but also business stakeholders who have a vested interest in the effectiveness of your organization's online efforts. They have a role to play as well.

Unfortunately, digital program management responsibilities are sometimes minimized or dismissed by digital leads that come from a hands-on digital development background. They focus the core digital team on production, possibly jumping in and playing a hands-on role themselves, while pushing aside practical management tasks. The result of this hyper-focus on production means that the digital team staff often suffers from a lack of professional development. Many Web managers and digital directors have only worked in digital and are unaware of tried-and-true human resource management tactics that could support and grow their staff. To add to the confusion, the human resource staff is often locked in a pre-Web worldview of canned marketing and IT job descriptions and is not able to effectively support the appropriate resourcing of the new field of digital. In a healthy environment, human resources departments, Web managers, and digital directors work together to manage and develop the digital team staff so that they have the same sort of career growth opportunities as those in marketing, sales, or IT.

Core Team Product Management

NOTE PRODUCT MANAGEMENT RESPONSIBILITIES

- Supervises product development and maintenance.
- Assists in Web development of community support and training.
- Gathers digital metrics.
- Informs digital policy.
- Defines digital standards.
- Implements and supports core infrastructure technologies.
- Develops and maintains the organization's "corporate" or top-level website.

The core team's product management arm is responsible for ensuring that the organization's *entire* digital system works coherently on many different levels. That includes technology platforms and content strategy, but also the "meta" aspects of development that give digital its power, like information architecture and taxonomy. This diversity of mission means that the core digital product management team serves as a digital domain expert, a service provider, an integrator, and a business analyst—all at the same time.

The product management arm of the core team is often responsible for defining digital standards and providing domain expertise in the definition of policy. They are also responsible for implementing strategies and technologies to support the measurement of digital effectiveness. Resources on this team help define the specific metrics and implement the processes and technologies for digital effectiveness measurement. They are also responsible for ensuring that shared aspects of digital are effectively managed and that other people in the organization who need to use those systems are properly trained to do so. That means that things like Web content management systems, analytics software, search engine software, ecommerce engines, and marketing automation software are often implemented and supported by this core team.

In practice, the core team is responsible for the tactical management of an organization's core digital presence, such as the main organizational website or the top-level pages of that site. See the "Core Team Roles" for a better understanding of the potential members of the core team.

NOTE CORE TEAM ROLES

- Application developers
- Content strategist
- Data analysts
- Developers
- Editors
- Graphic designers
- Information architects
- Librarians
- Producers
- Program managers
- Project managers
- Records managers
- Scrum manager
- Social media moderators
- Systems administrators
- Technologists
- Trainers
- Translators
- User experience specialists
- Videographers
- Writers

Should the Core Digital Team Be in Marketing or IT?

This is my most frequently asked question. There are usually two dynamics behind the question. The first is the desire to resolve a power struggle between certain organizational factions. The second dynamic is an assumption that there is an absolutely ideal structure and ideal home for all digital teams. That's not really the case. Good digital team design is always relative to a variety of factors, including how an organization budgets for digital, the geography of digital resources, and an array of other factors I'll discuss in Chapter 6, "Five Digital Governance Design Factors."

It doesn't matter if the core team is in marketing/communications/PR or a more technically focused team, like IT or IS. Either will work if roles, responsibilities, and funding are clear—and the team is complete. "Complete" means that all the resources required to support the development of digital are on the same team and reporting to the same manager. Often, companies will have split teams, meaning that all the design and editorial aspects are being dealt with by the communications or marketing team, and the application design and network and server infrastructure work is being handled by IT.

Keeping the Core Whole

Because of the core team's foundational role, ideally, it should not be scattered across multiple aspects of the organization. But, in practice, this is often not the case. In many organizations, the core digital team is bifurcated—with one main branch in the IT department and the other main branch in marketing, communications, or public relations. The reasons for this common split are obvious: a digital presence is a content-rich communications-focused series of channels that exist on a technology platform. Sometimes, in organizations with a transactional focus, the split can be two- or three-fold with other key stakeholder's organizations playing a strong core role.

Organizations should make an effort to overcome these legacy patterns and integrate digital resources on one team. Collaboration models where teams are distributed across the organizations and reporting to multiple managers can work, but for the core, it's especially important to foster close, spontaneous, and inventive collaboration—like that of the jazz ensemble—and this is best served when resources are co-located.

The Dispersed Core

If you work in a large organization or an organization that has vastly different product or business interests, the responsibilities of the core team may need to be dispersed. In these instances, multiple cores take on the same program and product management responsibilities as the corporate core team but for only a particular aspect of the digital presence, like an area of the organizational website or a brand-focused site or microsite.

For instance, in a holding company that has multiple brands and multiple websites, the core digital team's standards decision-making may be minimal with the bulk being delegated to individual brands or businesses. Sometimes, this delegation of authority can be so complete that the brand- or program-focused teams have complete authority over all the content, applications, and back-end systems that support digital. Another rationale for distributing core team functions might be localization requirements. While digital content is often translated from one language to another, sometimes digital products and services must be more deeply localized to align with business and cultural norms.

Often, in these deeply dispersed models, various brands, products, and programs have developed their own local digital governance concerns. For example, a product line that has been given authority to develop standards for its own product might delegate standards development authority to different geographical regions. When practices like these begin to emerge, the organization begins to develop a governance structure that resembles a network array with nodes of authority delegated from the core to brands, programs, or product lines of the organization (see Figure 2.3).

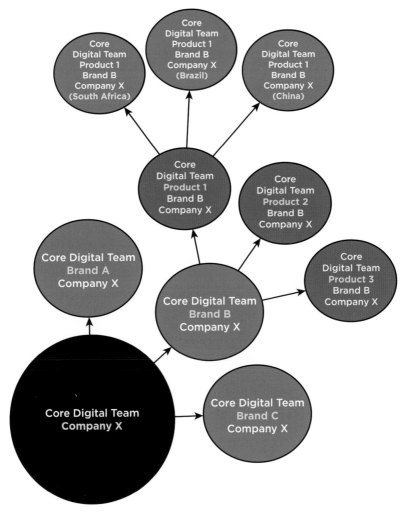

FIGURE 2.3
The dispersed core team.

This model, if well-designed, can be very powerful because it allows the top-level organization to dictate policy and standards in the areas where uniformity makes sense, while at the same time allowing brands and locales to have their own digital policy and standards as required to maximize business effectiveness.

The Clorox Company is an example of an organization where the vast majority of digital standards definitions (and corporate brand standards in general) might need to be delegated from the corporate core into specific brands. At the same time, some policy definition authority is still held at the Clorox corporate level (see Figure 2.4). Despite the variety of brands held by the Clorox Company, in the United States, most brands link back to the Clorox corporate site for their "Terms of Use" (see Figure 2.5). And a small amount of clicking around the Clorox Corporation brand-based website globally illustrates a complex array of digital standards and policies likely influenced by a difference in product offering and regional World Wide Web policy considerations.

FIGURE 2.4

The Clorox Company references its "Terms of Use" at the bottom of its page.

Terms of Use for United States Websites

Our Terms of Use for Canadian sites may be found here.

Last updated January 28, 2010

Your access to and use of our website(s) (the "**Website**") is subject to the following terms of use (these "**Terms of Use**") and all applicable statutes, orders, regulations, rules, and other laws. By accessing and browsing the Website, you accept and agree to be bound by these Terms of Use, which are conditions of permission to access the Website. If you do not agree to these Terms of Use, you may not have full access to the Website. If you are younger than 18 years of age, you are forbidden from becoming a member of the Website or posting information on the Website.

The form and nature of the services, content and all information posted on the Website is subject to change without notice. In addition, these Terms of Use may be changed, altered or modified at any time without prior notice. The Clorox Company ("**Company**," "**we**," or "**us**") will make such changes by posting them here. You should check this page periodically for such changes. You can determine when these Terms of Use were last revised by referring to the "LAST UPDATED" legend at the top of these Terms of Use. Your continued access of the Website after such changes conclusively demonstrates your acceptance of those changes.

We reserve the right, at any time and from time to time, temporarily or permanently, in whole or in part, to: modify or discontinue the Website, with or without notice; charge fees in connection with the use of the Website; modify and/or waive any fees charged in connection with the Website; and/or offer opportunities to some or all users of the Website. You agree that neither we nor any parent, subsidiary, or affiliate, nor any of our or their respective sponsors, vendors, licensors, or licensees (each, an "**Affiliated Entity**") shall be liable to you or to any third party for any modification, suspension or discontinuance of the Website, in whole or in part, or of any service, content, feature or product offered through the Website.

- Permitted Use, Limited License and Authorization to Reproduce
- Copyrights and Trademarks
- Unauthorized Use or Access
- Accuracy of Information You Submit
- Links To Other Sites
- Membership; User Names and Passwords
- Interactive Forums
- User-Submitted Ideas, Comments, and Other Content
- No Responsibility for Third Party Content
- No Confidentiality or Other Obligations
- Monitoring; Removal of Submissions
- Sweepstakes, Contests, and Similar Promotions
- Colors
- Product and Service Availability
- Shipping and Return/Replacement Policies
- Product Pricing
- Order Acceptance
- Termination of Access
- Privacy
- Disclaimer
- Disclaimer – ingredient, Natural, Processes, FAQs Content
- Indemnification
- Severability
- Waiver; Remedies
- International Users
- Filtering
- Contact Us; Questions or Complaints
- Digital Millennium Copyright Act Notice
- Governing Law; Forum
- Miscellaneous

1. PERMITTED USE, LIMITED LICENSE AND AUTHORIZATION TO REPRODUCE

Subject to these Terms of Use and any other terms and conditions on the Website, Company hereby grants to you the non-exclusive right to use the Website and download, install, reproduce, use and disclose the contents of the files or other media provided on the Website that are specifically identified as available for download, subject to the following conditions: (i) the material may be used for informational and noncommercial purposes only; (ii) it may not be modified in any way, nor distributed, transmitted or re-posted; (iii) no copy is made of any Company trademark or logo apart from the page on which it appears; and (iv) any copy of any portion of the material must include the copyright notice appearing on the Website. The Website, all of the information and materials contained herein, and the software used to make the Website available (collectively, "Content") are and shall remain the property of Company and its licensors and suppliers, and are

FIGURE 2.5

The Clorox Company's "Terms of Use" for United States websites.

Your Distributed Digital Team

NOTE DISTRIBUTED DIGITAL TEAM RESPONSIBILITIES

- Maintains the quality of a particular aspect of the digital presence.
- Develops and maintains content, applications, or data to support the digital presence.
- Provides input for the development of digital standards.

Once core standards and infrastructure systems are defined and implemented, a digital presence needs to be developed, supported, maintained, enhanced, and moderated. In large organizations, this is the responsibility of the distributed digital team. Using defined policy and standards as guidance, the distributed team extends and focuses the vision of the core team by implementing content and applications that map to specific business concerns.

In organizations with a relatively unsophisticated digital presence, the core team might oversee the maintenance and development of an aspect of the digital site like the main corporate website or top-level pages, but in an ideal model, the bulk of production and development should happen outside of the core. That model might mean product lines for business, admissions, and registrar's offices for universities, and membership and publications for non-profit organizations. This distribution makes sense because, while the core team may know best how its new functionality and content might fit into the overall organizational digital ecosystem, they can't be domain and knowledge experts regarding every aspect of the business. In organizations where digital governance is immature, distributing production among resources without a solid standards framework (and the authority to enforce it) will almost inevitably lead to a disintegrated user experience.

The scope of the day-to-day activities of the distributed team can be small or large. The responsibilities might include posting press releases on the public website or updating lunch menus on the intranet. Or your distributed team could implement applications and deploy new websites. The key point, as you'll see Chapter 5, "Stopping the Infighting about Digital Standards," is to put in place the authority for the standards definition. In most instances, the majority of that authority will lie within your core digital team, but sometimes that authority is passed on to the distributed Web team. For instance, authority for editorial standards might be delegated to the corporate entity that uses plain language standards, but other aspects of the organization that serve special audiences might allow a more specialized vocabulary for its user base. The important governance factor isn't where the work is being executed, but rather where the authority for the standards that control the outcome resides.

That designated authority doesn't mean that the members of the distributed digital team do not have a voice in the development of the standards they must comply with. You'll see in the standards chapter that they play a vital role in providing input for standards.

Committees, Councils, and Working Groups

NOTE THE ROLE OF COMMITTEES, COUNCILS, AND WORKING GROUPS

- Vets and approves guiding principles.
- Discusses high-level business metrics.
- Examines how digital should be resourced.
- Brainstorms new ideas or technologies.

An organization's digital presence represents an entire organization, so it only makes sense that cross-team collaboration and discussion will occur when developing and maintaining Web and mobile sites and moderating social channels. But sometimes organizations will have to form temporary and permanent working groups or committees to address certain digital concerns.

When these teams have a clear goal and mission, these committees, working groups, and councils can add real value to the organizational digital team. Production-focused "hands-on" groups make a great environment for digital standards decision makers to get input from stakeholders, and executive level steering committees are the natural home for vetting and approving guiding principles, discussing high-level business metrics, and having the tough conversations about how digital is resourced in the organization. Just make sure that you don't think these groups will take the place of a well-designed digital governance framework. Because they won't.

DO'S AND DON'TS

DO: Make sure that your working groups and committees are not substitutes for a real governance framework. Cross-functional working groups are wonderful for fostering collaboration, but sometimes they fail when it comes to establishing and enforcing standards.

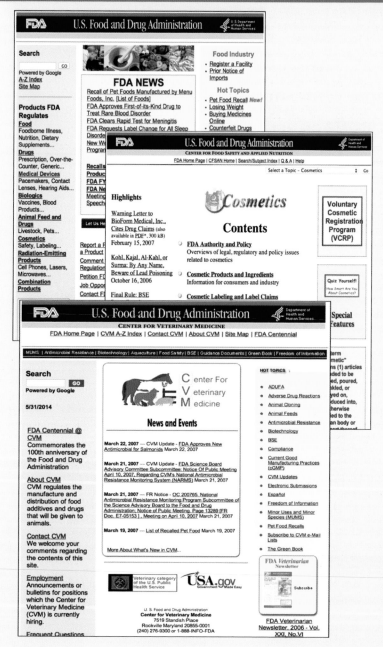

FIGURE 2.6

The FDA website circa 2007.

One of the early governance projects I worked on was with the United States Food and Drug Administration (FDA). The FDA, like many governmental agencies, leveraged the Web early in order to surface important information and data to citizens and specialized professionals. Within the FDA were multiple centers and to a certain degree, they all marched to their own drummer online. This resulted in a variety of different graphic designs online, sometimes making it unclear to users whether they were on an FDA site or somewhere else in the government (see Figure 2.6). Before executing the redesign, though, leadership took the extra steps necessary to establish a governing framework and established senior management level and executive level governing and working groups. The result was that the organization was able to move smoothly to a new integrated website design. Since then, the FDA has iterated on the design and functionality of its online presence, as shown in Figure 2.7.

FIGURE 2.7
The evolution of the FDA website.

Bridging resources are facilitators with no governing authority. Their job is to navigate horizontally and vertically within an organization in order to ensure production and goal alignment. Common bridge job titles are:

- Producers
- Scrum managers
- Project managers
- User experience experts

Bridges are patient negotiators who know your business, know digital, and can respect a deadline. In traditional organizations, these might be project managers. In interactive agencies, these could be producers. In an agile environment, they might be scrum managers. Whatever the name, the role of the bridge is vital. They are the "glue" between the requirements set or expected business outcome and the people who are getting the work done. Those people working in the bridging function move around a lot, and they go to a lot of meetings. They negotiate. As a group, they play the role of digital portfolio managers helping to prioritize projects and work for the organization. They interact with business stakeholders, developers, vendors—whomever they need to in order to get the job done.

In its essence, though, the bridging function provides two clear outcomes. First, it keeps the product management team focused on the business outcome, which means making sure that the functionality, system, and

Often, an organization's first attempt to address digital governance concerns is to create a governance-focused working group, council, or steering committee. More often than not, these groups are not able to effect the changes required in the organization, because they don't have any real authority. Pulling together a group of hands-on digital managers is a good idea if you want to brainstorm standards, educate, collaborate, or discuss best practices. However, a group of low-level managers usually doesn't have the authority to shift headcount or change an organizational budget. Alternately, executives who come together in a governance steering committee to approve digital projects usually don't have the digital expertise to make good decisions.

Your Extended Team

Because of the speed of change around digital, organizations are hard pressed to staff their teams with all the relevant skill sets, so leveraging external development and production expertise can content meet the business need, and that the project is delivered on time and within budget. Second, the bridges also keep the project business owner from bloating requirements ("scope creep") and from micromanaging and over-burdening artisan production resources so that these resources can do their work quickly and efficiently.

Organizations are notorious for not staffing this bridging function well. In many cases, artisan production resources are expected to do both the work and manage their internal "clients." This scenario is usually unproductive and can lead to bad situations where skilled digital resources spend most of their time in meetings and are forced to do their "real" job like developing code, designing, or writing content after hours or on weekends. And often, skilled digital artisans are not the best bridges. Traits like being hyper-focused and uncompromising, which might serve an application developer well, have a not-so-positive impact when the bearer attempts to function as a bridge. In many cases, the poor use of an artisan has led to conflict and staff fatigue. Sometimes, skilled and desirable resources move from one job to the next in search of relief when, in reality, the organization's expectations were simply unreasonable. In these cases, important information about the operations of the organizational digital platform leave with the resource, particularly in an environment where there are a lot of "homegrown" digital applications and systems that are largely undocumented.

make a lot of sense—particularly from a human and fiscal resource perspective. You should consider if it might make sense for your organization to utilize external vendor support. That support could range from simple overflow production support for a momentarily overtaxed internal digital team to the complete outsourcing of digital. Understanding who your external vendors are and how they support your core and distributed digital teams is important. Often, organizations have an array of vendors in place—sometimes working at cross-purposes. In these cases, the vendors are usually the last ones to tell the organization that their redundant services are not really needed, or worse, are not contributing to a higher quality experience for their users. You should have a firm understanding of which external vendors support your digital presence, what they do, and how much you are paying for their services. This list can include interactive agencies, as well as website hosting vendors, management and analytics consultants, software as a service vendors, systems integrators, and so on.

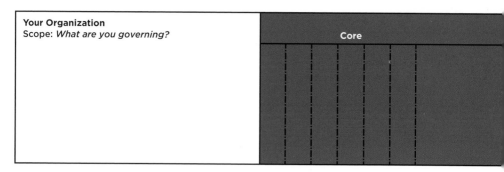

Your Organization Scope: *What are you governing?*	Core				

FIGURE 2.8

Your beginning digital governance framework fill-in-the-blanks.

Exercise: Establishing Your Field

Who is governing? Digital governance frameworks are organizational concerns (see Figure 2.8).

1. First, identify the organization that is delegating authority. It could be your top-level organization, or a branch, department, or some other organizational subdivision. Remember, if you are part of an organizational subdivision, it is import to ensure that you have the authority to delegate certain responsibilities. All authority is held at the core of the organization and then systematically delegated outward.

2. Describe the scope of your framework. Governance frameworks apply to a set of digital products and services, so it's important to be clear about what you are governing. Is it for all of your organization's websites, mobile applications, and social channels, or is it just your top-level site? If you have multiple digital properties and immature governance, even answering this question may take some conversation among stakeholders, particularly if there are websites and applications that the core team might feel are "rogue" or unsanctioned.

Dispersed Core				Distributed		Ad Hoc	Extended				

3. Identify the organizational components that function as your core, dispersed core (if any), distributed, ad hoc, and extended digital team members. At this point, just take a best guess. As you work through the rest of the book and examine strategy, policy, and standards decision-making authority in more detail, you may find that you need to make some adjustments. This is okay and normal.

Now that your field is outlined, you're ready to start allocating authority for decision making for digital strategy, policy, and standards.

SOFTWARE SELECTION AND GOVERNANCE

Alan Pelz-Sharpe, 451 Group

All too often, folks buy IT systems to solve a problem without fully understanding what the problem is in the first place. A proactive, up-front approach to digital governance provides an insight into what's really going on, and most importantly, provides a level of control that frankly is usually lacking in organizations. Buying software first, installing it, and then considering digital governance in retrospect will ensure more work and a much higher risk of failure.

Summary

- Your digital team includes the full spectrum of resources required to manage your digital presence. The team has four components: a core team; a distributed team; committees and working groups; and the extended team.

- The core team is responsible for defining and implementing the core digital platform and for establishing the standards that the entire team must adhere to.

- The distributed team is responsible for producing and maintaining an aspect of the digital presence. They bring business domain expertise or specialized knowledge to the digital presence.

- Committees, councils, and working groups add value by bringing together otherwise functionally silo'd resources in order to achieve a specific digital goal or to provide organization-wide oversight of digital efforts.

- The extended digital team includes non-employee resources that support your digital presence. This includes resources like website hosting service providers, interactive agencies, and technology implementation partners.

CHAPTER 3

Digital Strategy: Aligning Expertise and Authority

I take the train a lot from Baltimore to New York City. I'm not much of a train talker, but occasionally I will strike up a conversation with someone sitting near me at the end of my journey (see Figure 3.1).

WWW.SHUTTERSTOCK.COM

FIGURE 3.1
You can have some fascinating discussions en route.

Once, in the midst of an early evening approach to Penn station, New York, I started a conversation with a gentleman sharing my table in the café car. It was right around the time that Blockbuster (the global video brand) filed for bankruptcy and Netflix was starting to look super-savvy and invincible. The gentlemen had a *Wall Street Journal*, and I pointed to the Blockbuster story and said something like "Leadership sure dropped the ball on that one."

He put down his paper, looked at me over his glasses, and asked me what I did for a living. I told him, and he wrinkled his brow. (Okay, I don't have a normal job.)

"Have you ever heard of Clayton Christensen's concept of disruptive innovation?" He quizzed, taking on a teacher-like tone.

Of course.

"Well, he said, "When these sorts of disruptions happen, it's no one's fault. No one can see it coming. It's like a bomb dropping out of nowhere." *Wall Street Journal* back up in front of his face.

"Well," I said to the newspaper. "That would be true if this were the mid 1990s. But Netflix has been around for a while now, and Blockbuster must have noticed they were losing market share, right? So this was like a bomb you could see coming for 10 years."

No reaction. I continued.

"But I see this all the time in business. For whatever reason, management doesn't want to pay attention to obvious indicators. You know, there's a sort of managerial hubris that develops in successful organizations—where they somehow think they can't fail. Or they think they are *entitled* to majority market share, just because they've held it for so long."

Okay, so maybe I didn't say those exact words, but I did say something like it.

Paper down. "Managerial hubris?"

Oops.

The conversation went on a bit back and forth, and by the time we'd crossed under the Hudson and were getting off the train, it was clear that he and I were of two differing opinions. As an "executive at a publishing company," he felt that Blockbuster leadership had been blind-sided by the World Wide Web and "predatory" companies like Netflix, Redbox, and Amazon. I felt that executives should have seen the shifts in distribution channels coming a mile away and shifted their strategy to reflect the emerging new normal.

It didn't help our brief relationship that I also went on (I'd had one of those little mini bottles of wine) about the lack of deep and informed reaction to the World Wide Web in the publishing and media industry in general.

"So..." I asked, in parting, as we rode the escalator up into Pennsylvania Station. "Blockbuster leaders couldn't have made better choices?"

"Sure, here and there," he said emphatically. "But no one knows how all this technical stuff works. We're at the mercy of a bunch of kids fiddling around with our markets and changing all the rules."

And then he was gone.

The Organizational Response to Digital

In many instances, and in many different markets, senior leaders don't consider digital matters to be of strategic importance. For example, when I talk about digital to executives and their direct reports, they refer to websites, mobile channels, and social media as "technical stuff." Some leaders dismiss digital by saying, "I have staff that handles that." When asked about their digital budgets or performance measures, they often have no real answer. "I don't know," they say. "They tell me we get a lot of hits." Sometimes, if I strike up a real rapport with an executive, he might confide that he is completely confused or intimidated by this new platform—one that didn't exist when he built his career. How can he manage what he can't understand?

> **NOTE** DIGITAL STRATEGY DEFINITION
>
> A *digital strategy* articulates an organization's approach to leveraging the capabilities of the Internet and the World Wide Web. A digital strategy has two facets: guiding principles and performance objectives.

If interest in digital does exist, it might only be around the visual aspects of digital—the things they can see. Executives might think a competitor's website looks better, or they might covet a mobile app that they've downloaded on their smart phones. Occasionally, I'll get a leader who is a digital zealot. That opinion can manifest itself in a number of different ways, from a sensible well-supported digital strategy and execution plan (best) to random mandates to implement the functionality or application of the year (worst). (See "Is Your Leader a Digital Conservative or a Digital Progressive?" later in the chapter.)

Meanwhile, in the trenches, the digital team is often at a loss as to how to effectively make a strategic case for digital to executives. Maybe they've been trying for 10 to 15 years to get executives to fund their efforts and take digital seriously with varying degrees of success. The team has lobbied for big-ticket Web content management systems, search engines, and other software tools and asked for specialized headcount for things called *information architecture*, *Web analytics*, and *user experience*. When the Web teams are asked about leadership's role in digital, they might say that their executives are "ignorant" of the Web, old fashioned," "pre-digital," or "think that websites build themselves." These directors of digital, Web managers, and user experience experts usually say this with some disdain, because they feel that anyone who leads business in the 21st century ought to understand digital. Some even feel that "legacy" leadership needs to step aside and let the digital experts run the whole show.

This extreme dichotomy represents digital in a way that often resonates with digital workers: the digital team as a group of helpless marionettes dancing at the whim of a digitally clueless executive puppeteer. "*This* is why we can't develop a real digital strategy." But it's really not that simple.

Yes, there are a lot of executives who need to understand the impact of digital better, but some of an organization's inability to define and execute an effective digital strategy stems from the digital worker's lack of basic management skills. While senior leaders may have grown their careers in a pre-Web environment, leaving them less than Web-savvy, many digital workers have experienced their entire professional career in the rarified air of a corporate Web team. It's an environment that is often undervalued and understaffed, but one that also has a history of operating without clear performance objectives and accountability to the business.

Because digital teams are often led by managers who don't understand how digital works, digital resources may not have been developed as well as their counterparts in pure marketing or IT roles. So, even though the people may have worked in an organization for 10+ years and have tremendous responsibilities, they might not know how to write a budget, make a business case, negotiate with colleagues, or seek and offer mentorship. And it is these skills that are required in order to mature and integrate digital with the rest of the business.

DO'S AND DON'TS

DO: Make sure that your digital strategy is articulated via both quantitative and qualitative factors.

Luckily, senior managers and executive usually do have these skills in abundance. One of the benefits of properly identifying the resources that will define the organizational digital strategy is that there will, hopefully, be an intermingling of those people with institutional knowledge and business savvy and those with digital expertise—senior leaders and digital experts sitting in the same room having a serious conversation about how to get digital done in their organization. Hopefully, while the conversation is happening, some knowledge and skill transfer can take place.

Who Should Define Digital Strategy?

In Chapter 1, "The Basics of Digital Governance," you learned that a digital strategy team ought to have three types of people resources.

- People who know how to analyze and evaluate the impact of digital in your marketspace.

- People who have the knowledge and ability to conceive and design an informed and organizationally beneficial response to that impact.

- People who have the business expertise and authority to ensure that the digital vision is effectively implemented.

Usually, all three of these skill sets can be addressed if you put performance-focused leadership in the same room with your senior-most, "forest view" digital workers and user experience experts. Each of these resources has different skills and perspectives to add to the mix.

> **NOTE** THE ROLE OF LEADERSHIP
>
> A good leader should manage the following areas:
>
> - Make sure that the digital strategy is informed by non-digital strategic business objectives.
>
> - Ensure that the digital presence performs for the organization by pressing for and contributing to the definition of measure-able outcomes.
>
> - Provide market analysis and expertise, ensuring that the digital strategy is "worth the effort."
>
> - Align management for implementation of the digital strategy.

> **NOTE** THE ROLE OF THE DIGITAL WORKER
>
> The digital worker/user experience role should perform as follows:
>
> - Brainstorm and invent digital functionality in order to meet business goals.
>
> - Ensure that the digital presence aligns with good practices and relevant emerging trends in digital.

- Provide digital expertise and experience ensuring that the digital strategy is "doable."
- Ensure that the digital and non-digital experiences of the customer/user make sense and produce value for the business.
- Align organizational digital workers for implementation of the digital strategy.

Remember, the product of a digital strategy development is a statement of the organization's approach to digital and the development of performance measures—not a tactical plan. A digital strategy gets handed off to your team of digital leadership and stakeholders and workers (middle management and digital practitioners), who will figure out the best way to achieve those objectives (see Figure 3.2). So you don't have to fill the room with your whole Web team and every manager who has a stake in the digital strategy.

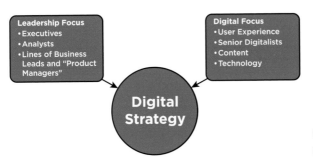

FIGURE 3.2
Digital strategy inputs.

In fact, if you include resources who know too much about how to execute on digital or feel too strongly about a single aspect of the business, a strategic conversation can quickly get bogged down in the tactics of how many websites, mobile apps, and social channels there are and what they'll do, or how to correct and fix the mess that you currently have online. Your team will be able to figure that out easily, once the strategy team defines what objectives the organization is trying to achieve online and once your digital governance framework clearly defines the roles and responsibilities for execution.

If your organization has a very small digital team, then your Web manager might be the *only* digital expert in the house. If this is the case, it's important for that person to take off his execution cap and focus on the strategic aspects of digital for the organization. In some cases, organizations may have no in-house strategic digital expertise. Perhaps they have outsourced all of digital to an external vendor. While this is sometimes an intentional move, it is more often a reactionary maneuver by leadership that doesn't want to deal with staffing for digital. While there are definite advantages to outsourcing certain aspects of digital, digital strategy isn't one of them. Even if your digital strategy team is populated with some external vendor experts, make sure that it is led and "owned" by the organization. If you don't have a resource that can do that, then hire it. It's a deficit you can't afford.

DO'S AND DON'TS

DON'T: Confuse your organizational digital strategy with your content, technology, or user experience strategies.

Do You Really Need a Separate Digital Strategy?

Sometimes a digital strategy might be so close to your organization's overall strategy that it might not be articulated separately. For instance, often digital *is* the product or service (think Amazon or Netflix). Then there are heavily impacted industries, like traditional print publishing and entertainment—ones that have already shifted or are shifting to an all or near-all digital product delivery model. In these cases, old paradigms have broken down, and there is an active business battle happening—the outcome of which will determine the new normal (see Figure 3.3).

If you work in one of these marketspaces, you're reeling right now. But you have also been given a gift, in a sense. Competition and the market have forced your organization to address digital strategy head-on. So, if you are someone whose job it is to manage digital in your organization, your job is dynamic and interesting. Hopefully, your organization has clarified whose role it is to define the strategy—most likely a diverse team that includes senior digital subject matter experts and business experts. In the best of cases, the organization has blended the legacy business strategy and operations with digital efforts so that everything works in concert.

FIGURE 3.3
The old business models are changing and new ones have surfaced.

> **DO:** Make sure that business experts *and* digital experts inform your digital strategy. Alone, neither of these resource types has enough knowledge to get the job done well.

The one-two punch of digital expertise and business acumen is a powerful combination, and when a digital strategy is defined with the combined knowledge of digital capabilities and business and market knowledge, a lot of profitable innovation can occur. For example, consider the way that Nordstrom reinvented its Web-based technology to surface inventory in all of its stores to customers shopping on the Web (see Figure 3.4). By doing so, Nordstrom relieved the company of inventory that in a pre-Web environment might have been left unsold, and yet, they also satisfied the customer's need in a single transaction. It took knowledge from both the pre-Web business experts and Web technologist to get this work done.

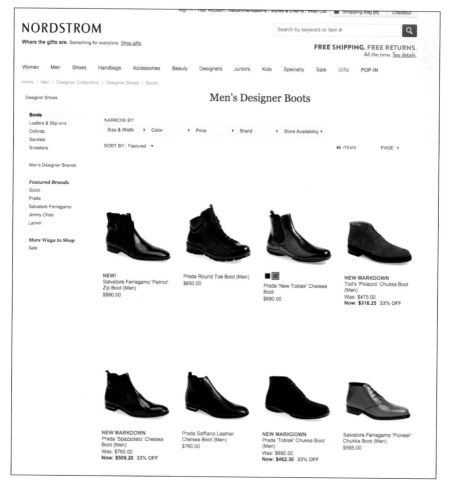

FIGURE 3.4
Nordstrom uses the Web to its best advantage.

What about organizations that have more subtly or ambiguously been disrupted by digital? What if you manufacture and distribute thermostat parts? What if you make ice cream? Often, conversations about digital center on businesses that have been heavily and publically disrupted—the obvious cases. So how do you determine your digital strategy when you are not *forced* to do so in order to remain viable or if the impact is more subtle? What happens if you see digital coming, but you just don't know exactly how it's going to impact your marketspace? Or what if most of what you do online happens behind your firewall on your intranet?

Interestingly, the majority of those businesses that I work with that have some of the most challenging governance concerns have not yet realized a real negative fiscal impact because of digital. They know that digital is there, but they haven't been forced by revenue to look *holistically* at their organizations and re-engineer them from the core because of digital. For instance, businesses in the pharmaceutical industry often have many, many product-focused websites of not the best (read "low") quality and some extreme governance concerns, but from a revenue perspective, these companies are some of the most profitable in the world and are doing very well. Sometimes the digital team in environments such as these ask me why their digital strategy isn't given more prominence. If digital strategy and business strategy are such close relations, they ask, why don't we just follow the lead of more heavily disrupted businesses and integrate digital strategy with the existing business strategy?

To be clear, I *do* believe that the integration of digital and "analog" business processes needs to happen, but in some cases that integration can be managed more gently. This is sometimes frustrating to those who work in digital for two reasons. First, digital experts often want to do some cutting-edge work, and sometimes they might be working in an organization that doesn't need to be that cutting edge about digital (at least at the moment). In that case, the individuals might want to consider whether or not that organization is a good vocational fit for them. Second, often organizations use the reality that their vital business systems were not disrupted by the Web as an excuse *not* to manage or govern digital at all. That's not good either. Every organization has a responsibility to ensure that their digital applications, website, and social channels are of good quality, represent their brand well, and are operating within the bounds of the law. And the first step toward these goals is defining a digital strategy. Having a strategy in place means that you will be intentional about the digital face of your organization. You will also be actively measuring the complex set of variables that will help inform executives and their teams when it is time to make a strategic move—so you don't end up like Blockbuster.

Measuring Performance in the Digital Age

Most digital workers understand Clayton Christensen's definition of disruption as outlined in his book *The Innovator's Dilemma: The Revolutionary Book That Will Change the Way You Do Business.* One of the key points Christensen makes is that leaders in marketspaces that have been disrupted often continue to use the legacy business metrics to measure their performance. Their narrow, dated view of their market might mean they overlook or discount new business indicators as they arise, particularly when it comes to digital. Digital brings to the table a mass of quantitative data available for businesses to analyze and new toolsets to gather that data.

The quickly growing field of digital analytics seeks to integrate old and new methods of data analysis. For example, it takes into consideration both traditional and well-known performance indicators, such as units sold and customer attrition and retention, but it also mines the log files of search engines, Web content management systems, and digital analytics tools for new data so that new indicators can be established. Today, organizations are talking a lot about "big data," specifically referring to this new data and the emerging methods of analysis available to organizations to better understand and fine-tune their business tactics.

Phil Kemelor, a thought leader in digital analytics, has outlined a number of areas that should be considered when defining digital metrics.

Web and Mobile

- Visitor activity
- Content and function usage
- Site promotion and marketing
- Internal search
- Task completion
- Site usability
- External search

Social

- Fans/followers/subscribers
- Traffic (visits, impressions/views)
- Interactions (likes, comments, posts, tweets, impressions)
- Channel ad campaign cost
- Sentiment
- Share of voice
- Value (or other research-based metrics)
- Referred traffic from social to Web or Web to social
- Referred conversions (or other online successes) from social to Web

Site Quality and Performance

- Standards compliance
- Server response time
- Server availability

Is Your Leader a Digital Conservative or a Digital Progressive?

Some organizations have a hard time getting leadership actively involved as a sponsor in the digital strategy, particularly when profit margins are healthy and the business has not been directly disrupted by the rise of Internet-enabled products and services. It's easy to attribute the apparent digital indifference of executives to digital ignorance. But, sometimes, whether an executive leans in to or leans away from digital has to do with the individual's personal perspective on digital. As with other aspects of business, leaders often are predisposed to a conservative or progressive approach to digital.

Digital Conservatives

Digital conservatives are slower to leverage the capabilities of digital to augment existing or invent new business processes, products, and services. Sometimes digital conservatism is adopted after a leader has analyzed the impact of digital on the business and come to the conclusion that, at least for the moment, being aggressive or innovative around digital is not of strategic importance. Or, perhaps, the organization has other, more strategic priorities. Other times, digital conservatism is the result of naiveté on the part of leaders—possibly an unsupported view that digital isn't important because it's not in the knowledge set of leaders, or is otherwise perceived unimportant.

DO'S AND DON'TS

DON'T: Expect digitally conservative leaders to eagerly adopt new technologies. Learn how to use metrics and more traditional business jargon to engage them in digital initiatives.

So it is often hard to determine which type of digitally conservative leader you might have. Those who are intentionally conservative about digital might still use traditional business metrics and tactics to evaluate their business. For example, they may notice that they are losing marketshare, but instead of stepping back and looking at the fundamentals in considering the changes that the disruption might have put on their organization, they react tactically in the same manner that they did in the predigital environment, not really understanding that the basic playing field of their business may have changed.

If a digitally conservative leader uses good management practices, intentionally delegates authority for digital strategy to more junior resources, and clearly establishes decision-making authority and organizational structure around digital development, then an organization led by a digital conservative might have a simple, small, and well-governed digital portfolio but one that is of the highest quality and very effective. If, on the other hand, a digital conservative is simply ignoring or dismissing digital without addressing the management mechanisms, the result could be and often is combating digital teams and online websites and social channels in disarray.

> **NOTE** THE UNINTENTIONAL DIGITAL CONSERVATIVE
>
> The unintentional digital conservative often has the following characteristics:
>
> • Delegates digital strategy to more junior resources due to lack of interest.
>
> • Feels threatened by digital.
>
> • Uses traditional pre-Web business metrics and tactics to evaluate and drive their business.
>
> • Is often unfamiliar with the strategic capabilities of digital.

> **NOTE** THE INTENTIONAL DIGITAL CONSERVATIVE
>
> The intentional digital conservative usually exhibits these characteristics:
>
> • Purposely delegates digital strategy to more junior resources.
>
> • Monitors how digital is impacting the organization.
>
> • Incorporates new ways of measuring business effectiveness.
>
> • Understands the strategic capabilities of digital and how it might be leveraged in the organization's market.

Digital Progressives

Digital progressives are faster to leverage the capabilities of digital to augment existing or invent new business processes, products, and services. There are obvious digital progressives, such as leaders of organizations like MailChimp, Amazon, and the myriad of other 1990s and more recent digital start-ups—organizations that built themselves from the ground up on a digital platform. All digital—

all the time. These organizations are obviously led by digital progressives. But if you look at organizations that existed prior to the advent of the commercial Web, you will see other dynamics.

In businesses that existed prior to the advent of the commercial Web, you will see two types of digitally progressive leaders. There are those out front who are reinventing their business and sometimes their vertical marketspace by maximizing the capabilities of digital. They might be leveraging "big data" to better understand the behaviors and needs of their customer base and to shape and drive the operations of the business. And you can also see the digital progressive that leans into digital indiscriminately. These people identify the latest digital technology or marketing tactic as a panacea or a quick boost onto the Internet, without paying attention to the fundamentals of real business needs and performance.

As with digital conservatism, an organization led by a digital progressive can have a positive or negative result. A progressive approach to digital with an undefined or ill-defined digital strategy and weak governance and operational practices can lead to chaos online. However, a progressive approach to digital with a clearly defined digital strategy and a clear approach to operations and governance can not only produce a great result for an organization, but it can also alter a marketspace.

NOTE THE UNINTENTIONAL DIGITAL PROGRESSIVE

The unintentional digital progressive might have these characteristics:

- Implements digital capabilities without real business case or performance objectives.
- Sometimes indiscriminately adopts new technologies without any real business purpose.

NOTE THE INTENTIONAL DIGITAL PROGRESSIVE

The intentional digital progressive often exhibits the following characteristics:

- Integrates digital strategy with overall business strategy.
- Utilizes digital capabilities to invent new ways to do business and to set norms for others in their marketspace.
- Tunes operational and governance practices to support the new normal of digital.

Whether your leader is a digital conservative or a digital progressive is not a case of "good" or "bad." It all depends on your organization's market and how digital is impacting that marketspace. For instance, might Blockbuster have done better with a digital progressive at the helm? Does your local plumber need to implement an application so that you can use your smart phone to make an appointment to get your sink unclogged? Does an engineering company need to capture the knowledge of its aging and retiring workforce?

These are strategic business decisions that point to the importance of a solid digital strategy informed by the knowledge and authority of digital experts and organizational leadership.

DIGITAL GOVERNANCE MATRIX

David Hobbs

Website migrations are complex and often result in a site that has the same problems that were in place before the transformation. Solid Web governance helps to define the website vision in the first place to anchor decisions in planning and executing the migration, take a longer and ongoing view of your website so the website quality doesn't immediately degrade after launch, clarify decision making so that important goals get more attention than the squeaky wheels, and also set the processes and structures to define standards so that the newly-migrated site is more consistent and coherent than the existing site.

Summary

- Organizational leadership and organizational digital team professionals often have different ideas about how the organization should adopt digital functionality. Sometimes leaders, particularly those who built their careers prior to the advent of the commercial WWW, are slow to explore digital capabilities. And, sometimes, digital professionals want to implement new technologies without a real business case for doing so.

- Defining an effective digital strategy requires both organizational and digital domain expertise. In the best case scenario, these two sets of resource work together, and in the process, have a knowledge exchange that can strengthen the skill sets of both leaders and digital domain experts.

- Not every organization needs a distinct digital strategy. In cases where digital products and services make up the vast majority of the organization's product and service offering, the digital strategy and business strategy can be the same thing. In instances where there is not an obvious way to leverage digital in order to benefit the organization, a separate digital strategy might be required.

Staying on Track with Digital Policy

G o to the website of a major organization. Now, scroll to the bottom of the page and look at the footer. Usually, the website footer is the domain of digital policy, as shown in Figure 4.1. That's because in many organizations, website footers are where you will find a link to the privacy statement and some sort of terms-of-use. There may also be a link to digital security, copyright, and accessibility information. Most often, when reviewed, users will see that these are actually digital policy statements—promises and intentions articulated by the organization regarding their online behavior. Sometimes the statements take the tone and complex language structure of a contract. Sometimes they are written in plain language. And sometimes both are true.

The website footer is often the home of some digital policy.

FIGURE 4.1
You can find policy references in the footer of Harvard's website.

Although privacy, security, accessibility, and copyright are important policy topics, they are really only the tip of the iceberg when it comes to digital policy (see Figure 4.2). But, for many organizations, these few statements resting in perpetuity in the footer reveal the full extent of an organization's attention to digital policy. That's unfortunate because the domain of digital policy is much broader than these few statements, and it extends beyond technical and communications concerns to broader corporate policy concerns, such as records management, intellectual property, and branding.

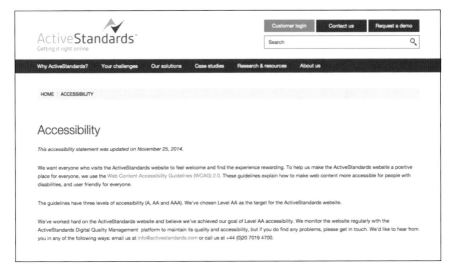

FIGURE 4.2
It's important to state your website's accessibility policy somewhere.

Finding Your Digital Policy

There are three main areas of digital policy that an organization needs to examine to ensure that their policy is complete:

- **Policies that are *new* to an organization because of the advent of the commercial Internet and World Wide Web.** Examples of these sorts of policies are social media and domain naming policies.

- **Policies that existed *prior* to the advent of the Internet and World Wide Web (WWW), but have been substantially impacted by these platforms.** Examples of these types of policies are accessibility and privacy policies.

- **Corporate policies that may appear to be *unrelated* to digital, but may need to be revised due to tacit assumptions.** Examples of these might be records retention policies where the legacy policy authors may have assumed that information dissemination would take place via paper or fax. The advent of the WWW has likely introduced new information dissemination practices, and therefore, some policies will need to be revisited and likely revised in order to ensure that they take into consideration any new risks and opportunities due to the use of online channels.

Often, organizations only tackle the first two of these three categories because the policy effort is driven by digital managers or IT resources that have a limited perspective. For instance, marketing and communications resource teams are very tuned into digital policy and standards concerns, but they not as aware of other types of risk associated with operating online, such as the impact that creating new website content might have on a corporate records retention policy that specifies what information needs to be kept for how long (and in what format) within an organization.

At the other end of the spectrum, there is the technical team. Their view of Web and mobile sites is generally hardware and software-focused, and more specifically about the reliability and security of such. So their perspective might cover a policy on the use of "cookies" and tracking devices, security, domain name management, and so on.

Some organizations will need to dive deeper or further categorize policy based on their business needs. For instance, organizations that support a digital presence of interest to children may have a specific children's online privacy policy, or those businesses in healthcare may need to address patient and medical information privacy concerns directly. Sometimes, multiple policies might have to be drafted to address certain geographic regions.

DO'S AND DON'TS

DO: Remember that digital policy extends beyond the usual copyright, terms of use, and privacy policy that can be found in many website footers.

Policy Is Boring and Standards Aren't

While many digital workers like to debate and discuss digital standards (see Chapter 5 "Stopping the Infighting About Digital Standards"), particularly those related to graphic design and information architecture, few of them are rushing to debate the nuances of digital policy. There are a couple of reasons why:

- **Digital policy can be perceived as boring and off-task.** For most staff involved with websites and social channels in an enterprise, discussing digital policy is not as interesting or exciting as discussing digital standards. Take your pick. Do you want to talk about the design for the new website or the Web records retention policy? Or do you want to deploy new social media applications on your intranet or talk about the social media policy for employees? Of course, there are those resources, such as enterprise records managers, human resources, or your in-house legal department, whose job it is to discuss and detail these concerns, but they are usually not front and center in the organization—let alone integrated into digital developments concerns.

- **Interest and expertise don't always intersect.** Those people who are most likely to be interested in managing risk for the organization, like a compliance, legal, or auditing department, are not usually the most Web–aware in the organization. Likewise, those people who are in a position to understand the risks inherent in operating online, such as digital managers, user experience architects, and applications developers, are not always organizationally savvy enough to communicate these risks to senior leadership—let alone define policy. So, even when there is significant risk due to a lack of digital policy, identifying that risk and addressing it can often be a task that is left undone.

Because of these two dynamics, many organizations just stick to the bare minimum as it relates to digital policy, where the digital team pushes policy development aside in favor of the "real" or more personally engaging work of defining digital standards. That's a mistake for two reasons:

- Policies help protect the organization from loss of revenue, relevance, and reputation due to unfavorable or illegal online activity. (Read: If you mess up here, you may not have a job.)

- Policies enable targeted and beneficial digital development by providing fundamental parameters for digital development.

Policy achieves these two goals by specifically including or excluding certain behaviors and developmental activities of the organization. For example, it's all right to have an organizational Twitter account, but if you are the social media moderator, *don't* air your personal political views on that account. These types of constraints might seem obvious or the sorts of things that an organization might be able to take for granted, but in my experience, all sorts of things *can* and *do* happen on organizational websites and social channels. While it's important to allow employees to have a level of autonomy in getting their digital work done, it's also important to consider and manage the risks that might really impact an organization's viability. That's the job of digital policy.

DO'S AND DON'TS

DON'T: Try to turn a policy into a standard. Policies should not contain design specifications and code snippets. Manage the risk with the policy. Leave protocols to the standards arena.

Policy Attributes

A policy is by nature general, and it identifies the corporate rules. The fact that it consists of brief statements does not mean that it is unenforceable, because a well-written policy will explain why the rules exist, when to apply them, to whom they apply, and what the consequences are if the rules are broken. You should consider the following attributes when creating a sound and strong policy:

- **Contextual:** The policy should consider the corporation in the context of its regulatory industry and public perception, at the local, regional, national, and global level in which it operates. It should consider the regulatory and legal ramifications of operating digital communications in this outward-facing context.

- **Inclusive:** The policy should consider the impact of all audiences directly or indirectly impacted by the policy and involve interested parties directly. It also should consider the ability to adopt and comply with the policy. (Note: I often see incremental adoption of a policy and subsequently recommend remediation versus penalty consequences.)

- **Realistic:** The policy should have a level of realism associated with it. In other words, the policy cannot express such a high standard that it is so unrealistic that it will never be completely achieved by those tasked

- **Enforceable:** The policy should be written so that those responsible for policy compliance can actually measure its compliance. Codifying policy in such a way that an organization has no way of determining whether or not it is being adhered to by stakeholders only weakens the policy domain.

- **Rooted in Evidence:** A policy should be rooted in expert opinion and industry practices. Rooting policy in applicable legal findings and rulings further ensures that the organization is well protected.

- **Comprehensive:** The policy must be holistic and look beyond the digital boundaries to the organization's strategic objectives (and, at times, those of the parent company) to establish the legal, moral, and ethical foundation for the policy. Cross-organizational objectives may need to be reflected (example: the need for communications to broadcast information and for security to protect sensitive information from being broadcast), and thus collaboration must be established and the joining of interests adopted into the policy.

While all of these attributes will not be written into the policy, the policy embodies all of these attributes.

Identifying a Policy Steward

When establishing your digital governance framework, it's essential that a policy steward be assigned. The digital policy steward must be able to strike a balance between the benefits of mitigating organizational risk associated with digital activities and the benefits associated with capitalizing upon and exploiting digital channels for fiscal and mission-related gain. That means that policy stewards need to be able to take an objective and dispassionate view of digital. For this reason, corporate legal is often a natural home for digital policy stewardship, but certainly not the only one. There are other compliance-focused or risk-management focused areas of organizations that are equally well positioned to serve the role of policy steward.

Usually, hands-on digital workers aren't my first pick as policy stewards. Often, they are too apt to minimize the risks associated with online development and, more importantly, can be ignorant of legislation that may impact policy choices. That doesn't mean that digital workers should be excluded from policy. As you'll see later, they are integral to the policy authoring process.

> **NOTE** RESPONSIBILITIES OF A POLICY STEWARD
>
> The policy steward often has the following responsibilities:
>
> - Ensures that the organization establishes and maintains a full set of relevant policy.
> - Effectively disseminates policy to the appropriate stakeholders.
> - Rationalizes corporate policy and digital policy.
> - Monitors shifts in the external Internet, World Wide Web, and other vertically specific policy and compliance concerns.

> **NOTE** CHARACTERISTICS OF A POLICY STEWARD
>
> Most policy stewards exhibit the following characteristics:
>
> - Understands and applies laws and regulations related to the Internet and WWW to the organization.
> - Understands and interprets laws and regulation for the organization's market segment.
> - Understands high-level organizational objectives.
> - Acts as a mediator between various organizational interests with an objective viewpoint.

Despite the reality that corporate legal, on the face of it, appears to be a natural home for digital policy stewardship, in practice, legal departments and other aspects of "corporate" can be functionally detached from the digital policy stewardship process. Usually, this isn't a rejection of the role, but rather a maturity concern. Typically, a legal department is accustomed to weighing in on the footer polices mentioned earlier because they have an established relationship with the IT department that is focused on aspects of security and privacy, as well as a relationship with marketing and public affairs, which often oversee the substance of copyright and branding policy. But digital is still new enough that many of the more subtle implications of its impact on policy are in the legal department's blind spot.

So legal resources that typically would ensure proper risk management in other areas of the company don't necessarily know or understand the risks associated with digital. For instance, a legal department may not consider that the lack of a domain naming policy might mean that there are no standards in the organization regarding who is allowed to buy domain names (and subsequently put up Web and mobile sites in the company's name).

DO'S AND DON'TS

DON'T: Assume that your legal department will know when to step forward to address digital policy considerations. Often, the legal team lacks the digital expertise to identify when and where online risk exists.

In practice, I have worked with large, global companies that have no idea how many websites they have online or who is making content for them. That sort of behavior represents unmanaged risk. It's the role of the policy steward to ensure that digital risk is effectively evaluated and the range of policies defined in an organization is appropriate for managing that risk.

Assigning Policy Authorship Responsibilities

Policy authors must consider the variables that inform a policy (risk, law, regulation, and an organization's digital strategy) before they create an informed policy statement. At times, a single policy might require contributions from multiple authors. But, from a process perspective, it's important that there be an author "owner" who is committed to having the appropriate discussions with stakeholders and making the first attempt at drafting the policy.

NOTE RESPONSIBILITIES OF A POLICY AUTHOR

The responsibilities of a policy author encompass the following tasks:

- Speculates and interprets the impact of digital activities on the organization.
- Defines an organizational position on a particular policy topic.
- Drafts and maintains digital policy.

NOTE CHARACTERISTICS OF A POLICY AUTHOR

The characteristics of a policy author are the following:

- Liaises with organizational and digital subject matter experts to envision and articulate the tactical and organizational implications inherent in implementing certain functionality.

- Speaks of digital in "plain language."

- Understands the high-level implications of certain tactical digital development choices.

Because of the subject matter diversity of policy, authorship is usually distributed across the enterprise. If policy is being authored in a centralized manner from one vantage point of the business, there should be strong concerns that the full policy picture is not being considered. The informed opinions of legal, marketing, communications, technology, and Web experts, as well as business and programmatic resources, are needed to draft effective policies. Exactly where a specific policy is authored in the enterprise is subject to the peculiarities of an organization's history, structure, management style, and so on. For guidance, consider using the authorship responsibilities in Table 4.1 as a starting point.

Remember, policy might revolve around a particular competency or organizational concern, but it is meant to protect the interests of the entire organization. Policy authors should make sure that they consult with the right resources when necessary. Your legal department ought to be able to offer insight related to external legislation, regulation, or policy that may shape your organization's online behavior and point out links to and implications for other corporate policies, such as privacy, copyright, and records management. Marketing and communications resources are often the last word on corporate branding, including matters related to visual identity. Finally, technologists understand IT security, and digital experts are a wellspring of expertise when it comes to understanding the practical implications of digital functionality, including information architecture and keyword tagging.

TABLE 4.1 POSSIBLE POLICY AUTHORS

Policy Topic	Candidate(s) for Primary Author
Accessibility	Accessibility officer
	User experience architect
Branding	Marketing
	Communications
	Public affairs
Digital Records Management	Records manager
	Senior Web manager
Domain Names	Information technology, marketing, public relations
	Senior Web manager
	Compliance
Hyperlinks and Hyperlinking	Web team
	Information technology
	Communications
Intellectual Property Protection	Legal
	Compliance
	Branding
	Senior Web manager
Language and Localization	Communications
	Public affairs
	Legal
	Human resources (for intranets)
Privacy	Legal
	Information technology
Security	Information or security officer
Social Media	Senior Web manger
	Human resources

In my experience, when policy is segregated from the more tactical struggles around standards definition (like the look and feel of a website homepage), debates about the substance of the policy are minimized. That's because most digital stakeholders aren't interested in risk; instead, they are interested in what their websites look like and where their content is on the site. However, sometimes there are debates about how much risk an organization should be willing to take when operating online or defining the organization's online identity. An example might encompass debates about the use of social channels. For example, what are employees allowed to say on behalf of the company and what are the consequences if an employee steps "out of bounds?" Or a policy debate could be about the interpretation of the law, because often national and local laws have not caught up with the realities of digital. Or the debates could be about the culture and values of an organization versus profitability (user privacy vs. using "big data" to your advantage). So, you'll often find ambiguity and real options that must be discussed before forming a policy statement.

Because of the impact of policy decisions, when there is a lack of consensus about the substance of the policy, those concerns are best escalated to the appropriate management level. Policy positions can and do impact the core of an organization's viability and culture. If there are debates in this area, they are best addressed by the people who hold accountability.

Writing Digital Policy

I've worked on projects where the corporate process for codifying policy was so troublesome that many of the people on the digital team just didn't do it. That's the wrong choice. I understand that impulse, but policy is too important—if only to inform the more resonant set of protocols: digital standards—and, as you'll see, everyone cares about digital standards.

Many organizations have an existing process and template for drafting, codifying, and disseminating corporate policy. If digital policy is to be taken seriously by everyone in the organization, then the policy steward should ensure that this standard process and template are utilized—even if they are arcane. This might be repugnant to those who work in the user experience arena or to writers or Web managers who are used to just getting things done. But, if there is an opportunity to improve the process and template or to impact the quality and clarity of the policy communication, then go right ahead. Just don't stall the process of establishing digital policy in order to do so.

Whether your organization already has a framework for establishing policy or not, there are some good practices related to structure and content to consider.

1. **Use a standard format:** Policy by its nature is not necessarily an interesting read for most. So try to use a standardized document format for all digital policy so that your community knows where to look for information that is relevant to them. Components to consider are:

   a. **Policy title:** What is the policy about?

   b. **Policy summary:** What is the gist of the policy in plain language?

   c. **Related polices and standards:** What references to other policies and standards could be impacted?

   d. **Policy revision date:** When was this policy last updated?

   e. **Policy scope:** To what digital artifacts and products does this policy apply?

2. **Use language that people understand (not jargon):** Sometimes, after all the legal and regulatory concerns have been addressed with precision, corporate policy can be dense and difficult to comprehend for the average employee or customer. You've all read incomprehensible privacy statements on websites. The policy author should ensure that policy statements are summarized and communicated in a language that everyone understands (see Figure 4.3). In my experience, sometimes those who are most impacted by policy—the people who write the code and manage the corporate website—are the ones who are least informed about digital policy. Often, this situation occurs because the policy language is arcane and the applicability of the policy to everyday digital work is not clear.

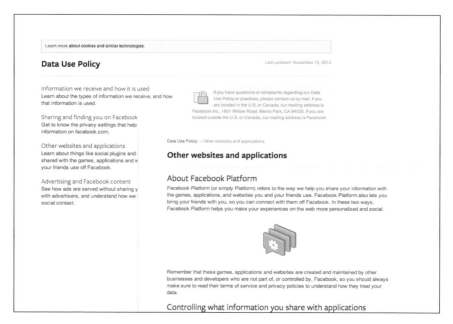

Learn more about cookies and similar technologies.

Data Use Policy   Last updated: November 15, 2013

Information we receive and how it is used
Learn about the types of information we receive, and how
that information is used.

Sharing and finding you on Facebook
Get to know the privacy settings that help
information on facebook.com.

Other websites and applications
Learn about things like social plugins and
shared with the games, applications and w
your friends use off Facebook.

Advertising and Facebook content
See how ads are served without sharing y
with advertisers, and understand how we
social context.

If you have questions or complaints regarding our Data
Use Policy or practices, please contact us by mail. If you
are located in the U.S. or Canada, our mailing address is
Facebook Inc., 1601 Willow Road, Menlo Park, CA 94025. If you are
located outside the U.S. or Canada, our mailing address is Facebook

Data Use Policy → Other websites and applications

Other websites and applications

About Facebook Platform
Facebook Platform (or simply Platform) refers to the way we help you share your information with
the games, applications, and websites you and your friends use. Facebook Platform also lets you
bring your friends with you, so you can connect with them off Facebook. In these two ways,
Facebook Platform helps you make your experiences on the web more personalized and social.

Remember that these games, applications and websites are created and maintained by other
businesses and developers who are not part of, or controlled by, Facebook, so you should always
make sure to read their terms of service and privacy policies to understand how they treat your
data.

Controlling what information you share with applications

FIGURE 4.3
Facebook uses ordinary language to explain policy.

3. **Be inclusive:** Remember, policy is meant to protect the organization, so the entire organization should be considered for input.
The policy perspective of an aspect of a business that operates
in Canada might be very different than the perspective of those
working in Spain. Your legal department ought to be able to
offer insight related to external legislation, regulation, or policy
that may shape your organization's online behavior and point
out links to and implications for other corporate policies, such
as privacy and copyright and records management. And your
digital team can illuminate exactly what is happening with information that is collected on sites and via various applications and
processes. Lines of business, product lines, or other organizational divisions also have a relevant viewpoint. They know what
they are trying to achieve from a fiscal and mission perspective—whether that's ramping up sales in a particular product
line or recruiting more students to a particular area of study for
a university, or something else. It takes a village to draft a digital
policy. So err on the side of inclusion instead of exclusion.

4. **Vet with the experts:** No matter who is consulted during the drafting, two areas should review any digital policy that is written: the core digital team and the legal department. The digital team should determine if the policy is realistic, given the reality of online tactics. After the policy has passed the digital team practicality test, its next stop should be legal—which often has the final set of recommendations for revision. Usually, there is a back and forth between the legal team and the digital team as they find the right set of constraints that will enable the enterprise to do business effectively online and protect the organization from litigation or other negative factors. Revision and negotiation are usually required at this point. Sometimes, when there are tough choices to be made, senior management or executives may need to weigh in on the matter to make a judgment about how much risk the organization is willing to take in order to achieve a certain goal.

5. **Formalize:** If it is to be complied with and otherwise taken seriously during the normal course of business, policy must be codified and disseminated to the organization. Many large organizations have a formal process for accomplishing this. Sometimes it involves assigning a formal policy document number and integrating it into the larger set of corporate policy. Sometimes the document just needs to be posted online on the employee intranet or on the website. In the most formal of situations, an executive signature may be required as well. The policy stewards, if well selected, should be aware of this process and shepherd any new or revised policy through the gauntlet of codification.

6. **Communicate:** Whatever your organization's codification process is, make sure that the policy creation process doesn't stop there. It's important that all stakeholders are aware of new and revised policy, especially if those stakeholders are the public (see Figure 4.4). Some areas, such as the website privacy, security, and accessibility policy, are easy to find because they end up in the footer of the website. But it's important to know where the more obscure policies are housed and make sure that those who are involved in digital development—the full digital team—know where those policies are located. Often, people find that locating existing digital policy is tantamount to conducting an unfruitful archeological dig on the organizational intranet. That's not a good thing.

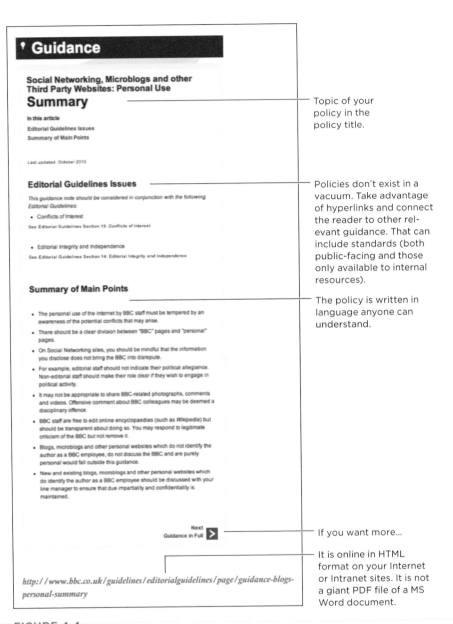

Guidance

Social Networking, Microblogs and other
Third Party Websites: Personal Use

Summary

In this article

Editorial Guidelines Issues

Summary of Main Points

Last updated: October 2010

Editorial Guidelines Issues

This guidance note should be considered in conjunction with the following Editorial Guidelines:

- Conflicts of Interest

See Editorial Guidelines Section 15: Conflicts of Interest

- Editorial Integrity and Independence

See Editorial Guidelines Section 14: Editorial Integrity and Independence

Summary of Main Points

- The personal use of the internet by BBC staff must be tempered by an awareness of the potential conflicts that may arise.
- There should be a clear division between "BBC" pages and "personal" pages.
- On Social Networking sites, you should be mindful that the information you disclose does not bring the BBC into disrepute.
- For example, editorial staff should not indicate their political allegiance. Non-editorial staff should make their role clear if they wish to engage in political activity.
- It may not be appropriate to share BBC-related photographs, comments and videos. Offensive comment about BBC colleagues may be deemed a disciplinary offence.
- BBC staff are free to edit online encyclopaedias (such as Wikipedia) but should be transparent about doing so. You may respond to legitimate criticism of the BBC but not remove it.
- Blogs, microblogs and other personal websites which do not identify the author as a BBC employee, do not discuss the BBC and are purely personal would fall outside this guidance.
- New and existing blogs, microblogs and other personal websites which do identify the author as a BBC employee should be discussed with your line manager to ensure that due impartiality and confidentiality is maintained.

Next
Guidance in Full ▶

http://www.bbc.co.uk/guidelines/editorialguidelines/page/guidance-blogs-personal-summary

Annotations (right margin):

Topic of your policy in the policy title.

Policies don't exist in a vacuum. Take advantage of hyperlinks and connect the reader to other relevant guidance. That can include standards (both public-facing and those only available to internal resources).

The policy is written in language anyone can understand.

If you want more...

It is online in HTML format on your Internet or Intranet sites. It is not a giant PDF file of a MS Word document.

FIGURE 4.4
An example of the BBC's policy with my annotations.

7. **Keep it up-to-date:** Digital policy (and standards) exist and serve a very specific role in an enterprise digital ecosystem. Sometimes the process for establishing digital policy can be considered a terminal, one-time process. But it's not. Your policy has to remain *accurate* over time. If your digital information practices change, your policy should change. For example, your privacy policy might need to change so that you do not use information collected under the earlier policy without getting permission (even if is implied) from those users.

    It is important to understand that policy stewards and authors must be vigilant, staying up-to-date with the implications of the latest technology and content trends to ensure that the policy is revised when necessary and continues to protect the interests of the enterprise.

8. **Retire at sunset:** Digital policy, like other artifacts, can become arcane and irrelevant. It is important to understand when it is no longer needed and retire it in favor of a new policy, or in some instances, no policy at all. Most often, you'll see the "sunsetting" of policy during mergers and acquisitions or a change in the regulatory operating environment. While infrequent, this stage is part of the policy lifecycle, and rather than simply updating it, you should always review the policy for its relevance and necessity.

DO'S AND DON'TS

DO: Think about policy that might be relevant for your particular marketspace—particularly if you function in a heavily regulated industry like financial services or pharmaceuticals.

Raising Awareness About Digital Policy

Whose job is it to initiate the process of digital policy development in your organization? In the early and immature stages, that answer is simple: If you see something, say something—even if you are the junior-most application developer or a graphic designer. If you see risk to the enterprise, raise your concerns. Websites, mobile sites, and social software interactions are still relatively new entities inside organizations, and you can't rely on those people who are higher up to be able to recognize and understand risk associated with doing business online.

If you are a junior-ish editorial resource in the public affairs department and you know that there are 17 social media accounts being moderated by people who aren't fully considering the viral nature of social media channels, and you know your organization doesn't have a social media policy about this behavior, bring it up. Get the conversation started. You don't have to be the last word on the matter, but you *can* be the first. Express your concern to those who have the authority to impact change. Try not to use a lot of technical or marketing jargon. The legal or compliance departments usually care about digital policy concerns, but often no one has taken the time to speak to them about the risks in a language they understand.

If you are a Web manager or digital director and want to help non-Web savvy resources understand the risks associated with certain online practices, use screenshots to show examples of redundant or outdated content on your sites and link that situation to the absence of a Web records management policy (and supporting standards). Or, if you are managing an intranet, consider communicating knowledge management concerns related to, say, the proliferation of largely unmanaged SharePoint instances on the intranet and how they might contain human resource-related information that may or may not be what your organization wants to communicate to its employees.

DIGITAL POLICY CONSULTANT

Kristina Podnar

Policy is intended to create a framework for behavior that is aligned with the governing body of an organization. If you want people to read (and follow!) your policy—whether they be website visitors or employees working on digital content—you should keep it short and written in plain language. You should state the "what" and "why" within several sentences, or a paragraph at most. Your goal is to clearly and quickly explain to the reader the impact on them as a result of using the digital content (for the website visitor) or how they should behave in creating the digital content (for the digital worker). If you find it necessary to document additional details, such as the "how" to execute within the context of a policy, you should develop a companion operating procedure.

Summary

- Policies exist to manage the risks associated with operating online. Your legal department, privacy and security officers, and digital experts will be integral in establishing an appropriate set of policies.

- When considering policy development, it's important to examine existing corporate policies, as well as IT and marketing-focused policies, that may have been impacted by digital. New polices may need to be written because of the advent of the Internet and the World Wide Web.

- Organizations should appoint a policy steward to ensure that the organization is drafting an appropriate set of policies and that the policy is properly codified in the organization.

- Policy authoring should be an inclusive process that leverages the varied skill sets of organizational stakeholders from IT, marketing, public relations, or divisionally focused entities.

- Make sure that you use a consistently structured format for authoring policy and that you write your statements in plain language and that your policies are properly vetted and codified according to organizational processes.

CHAPTER 5

Stopping the Infighting About Digital Standards

I grew up in Columbia, Maryland, a planned community (see Figure 5.1). And as with the word "governance," people tend to react to the phrase "planned community" in a not-so-positive way. "Planned" sounds dull and uncreative to people: cookie-cutter homes, on cookie-cutter lots, on cookie-cutter streets—"Little Houses Made of Ticky Tacky," to invoke Malvina Reynolds' well-known song. And Columbia was all about that: a city built quickly based on a template. There were street naming conventions, standard model homes, standardized lot sizes, and a standard "village" configuration complete with strategically placed shopping and swimming pools.

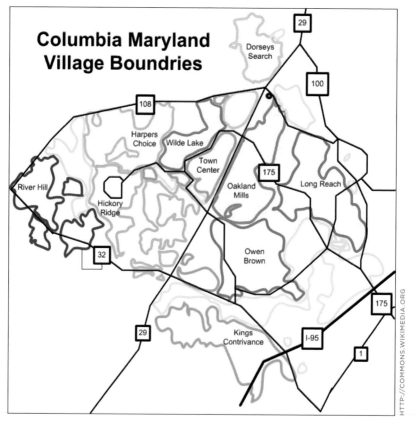

FIGURE 5.1

Columbia, Maryland—a planned community that opened in 1967.

So what do you get when you build a city on a standards-based framework? Those who focus on the standards part like to say "boring," "all the same," "not diverse," because they believe that any standardization leads to a lack of creativity or innovation. But that wasn't all there was to it. Once you factor in the context and intent of Columbia, the picture becomes different. Columbia was one of the first planned communities intended to be racially and economically integrated. Its founder, James Rouse, had a vision about creating a place for people to live—a place that would make you feel good, a place where everyone would just get along. And there was the timing: Columbia was founded in the mid-sixties and started its initial growth spurt in the 1970s.

In standardized fashion, villages and neighborhoods were often named after literary figures with streets being named after lines in their works. That standard resulted in street names like Evening Wind Lane, Wood Elves Way, and Plaited Reed. No Main Street. No Church Street. No School Street. Sure, there are some boring people in Columbia, but Columbia has spawned some interesting people, too, including the following:

- **The late Randy Pausch:** The Carnegie Mellon professor who gave us "The Last Lecture: Really Achieving Your Childhood Dreams." This one touched home, as his mother was an English teacher at the high school I attended.

- **Michael Chabon:** Pulitzer prize winning author. I like to think that Mike's rich writing style was informed by the literary tradition of Columbia street names. But that might be a stretch. I think he just has a gift.

- **Dave McClure:** Founder of 500 Start-Ups and a rule breaker if ever there was one.

- **Aaron McGruder:** Of Boondocks comics fame; another iconoclast.

- **Edward Norton:** Okay, he's just the grandson of James Rouse, but cool nonetheless. I mean, *Fight Club*, right?

All this is to say that, contrary to popular belief from some of my clients, standardization does not have to give way to things boring or flat or uninteresting. It doesn't mean that the standardized interface can't be beautiful, or that your customer's experience of your seamlessly integrated process that takes them from desktop to mobile to call center won't be sublime. The belief that standardization necessarily leads to the boring and uninteresting is too simple. It's what's going on inside the structure that is important. You could have a beautiful, old, organically grown, charming town with nothing creative going on for it except that it looks good. Or you can have tract housing turning out really interesting people, music, and thought. It's all about the substance and interactivity of the interior. What comes out of a community, planned or unplanned, is really contingent upon the intention and people within it.

DO'S AND DON'TS

DO: Remember that standards are normal. Most things operate within a standards-based framework. Find the right framework that will work.

So, if you're going to take the time to establish and implement a standards framework, it had better be around the right intention. And that intention is expressed through your digital strategy. Your standards are the tactical manifestation of your strategy that will bring into existence the intent of your digital strategy. That's why organizations that have no real digital strategy struggle so much with coming up with a quality online presence and why their digital team spends so much time arguing and debating about standards. In the absence of clear business intent, standards can be left up to a matter of taste and debate. So, if you are undertaking to develop standards without first having defined a digital strategy, you may develop a standards-compliant website and have consistently moderated social channels. But your digital target will likely not resonate as well as it could with your customers. Only standards derived from clear vision have the capacity to create a high user experience and deliver on the mission of your organization.

DO'S AND DON'TS

DON'T: Confuse freedom of speech with freedom from standards. Those are two different things.

I was lucky. I learned early that standards could enable rapid growth and provide a framework for coherent development, all the while creating a space for real creativity. Standardization can be, and often has been, the platform for creative and important work. But I'll go further. Standards, in fact, might be an essential ingredient. Standards frame and limit what you can do so that you can get across a certain message or get a particular piece of work done. And that's the message you should carry to digital teams who are reluctant to adopt a standards-based framework.

Likewise, you can have a World Wide Web operating within the open standards of the W3C with the whole of humanity trying to express itself freely and creatively, or you could have something else, like an Internet and Web controlled by a few businesses and political interests. It's about clarity of intention and the quality and sustaining quality of your implementation. It's about having a vision and figuring out how to make it happen and holding true to your aims and your standards.

Why Digital Standards Are Important

Practically speaking, having digital standards enables an organization to put into place details for execution so that digital work can be performed consistently and effectively. From a governance perspective, knowing who has the authority to define standards saves time by minimizing the time that resources spend making decisions about the same factors, over and over again. For instance, it's good to know which Web browsers your organization's digital presence supports, what fonts you use for mobile applications, and when and where it's acceptable to use your organization's mark. It might also be good to know that your organization operates on a .net platform, or that when you refer to staff on a public website it's always "Ms. Welchman" and not "Lisa."

In an ecommerce environment, standards make sure that the right content gets to the right customer at the right point in the sales cycle. For example, it's good for customers to know that whatever they are buying on a site, the sales checkout process will be the same. And it makes customers more comfortable knowing that whether they are purchasing a pair of trousers or a jacket, they will still have the same interface for toggling between garment color choices. In addition, it doesn't just make the user's task easier to accomplish, it also takes stress off internal digital workers.

Adopting a standards-based framework takes the stress out of development. When you have standards in place, more time can be spent having conversations about the substance and purpose of the work that is to be done instead of arguing about the details of execution or who has the authority to make decisions about application coding standards or a graphical user interface.

Many things that people value operate within a standards-based framework, as these examples and Figures 5.2-5.4 show: DNA, Julian calendar, TCP/IP, Equal Temperament, XML, Haiku, 24-hour clock, punch cards, alphabets, metric system, musical notation, and movable type.

FIGURE 5.2

Music is based on definitive standards.

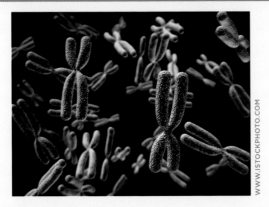

WWW.ISTOCKPHOTO.COM

FIGURE 5.3

Human beings are based on standards.

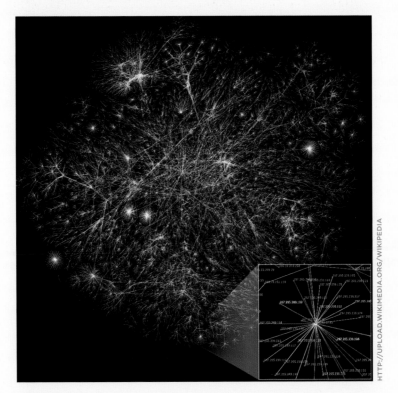

HTTP://UPLOAD.WIKIMEDIA.ORG/WIKIPEDIA

FIGURE 5.4

The Internet operates over a standards-based framework.

Identifying a Standards Steward

A standards steward should have the following characteristics:

- Should be a digital generalist.
- Have a "forest" view of the organization's digital presence.
- Have a librarian's head for organization

The responsibilities of the standards steward are the following:

- Ensure that the full standards lifecycle (see Figure 5.5) is addressed for each standard.
- Create and prioritize list of standards for definition.
- Develop a standard format for standards documentation.
- Measure and report on standards compliance.

An organization's digital standards steward's job is to establish and maintain a standards-compliant environment within the organization (see Figure 5.5). Standards compliance exists in an environment where certain activities have occurred:

- Standards have been defined and documented.
- Standards have been effectively disseminated to all digital stakeholders.
- Standards have been implemented.
- Standards compliance is measured and managed.

The reason why most organizations have trouble with standards compliance is because they miss or incorrectly address these activities and then are only left with one alternative—to enforce (usually undocumented) standards after the non-compliant content and applications are already posted (or nearly posted) online. This reactive dynamic can lead to a stressful dynamic for digital teams. Too often, the core digital team is perceived as the last-minute bad guy, telling teams that the look and feel isn't right or that the flow of the application screens is unusable.

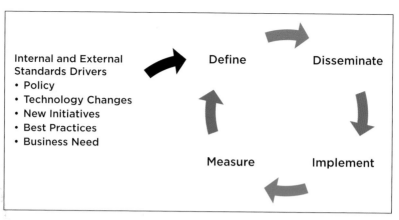

FIGURE 5.5
Creating a standards-compliant environment.

The core digital team shouldn't be in the position of having to ask their colleagues to remove content and applications that might represent weeks or months of effort. In the best of cases, the organizational standards steward is not an enforcer, but someone who is able to create an environment where bad things don't get online in the first place. Let's take a look at what the standards steward does to make that happen (see Table 5.1).

DO'S AND DON'TS

DO: Make a distinction between policies, standards, and guidelines. Each of these serves a different purpose—to protect the organization, ensure online quality, and guide tactical behavior, respectively.

NOTE PROCEDURES

Procedures (also known as *standards operating procedures*) are as important as policies, standards, and guidelines. In practice, procedures are used as a medium for conveying execution requirements in an organization. While policy and standards define basic constraints and specific protocols for digital development, a procedure outlines exactly *how* to execute policy and standards. When policy, standards, and procedure are effectively teamed, they provide a clear and concise direction necessary for consistent digital operation.

TABLE 5.1 IS IT A POLICY, A STANDARD, OR A GUIDELINE?

	Policy	Standard	Guideline
What is its function?	To manage organizational risk associated with operating online	To specify development protocols	To steer resources into making the "correct" decision in a subjective context
What does it protect?	The enterprise	The quality and effectiveness of the digital presence	Digital quality and organizational norms
Who codifies and maintains it?	Legal; senior management or compliance division; board; human resources	Digital subject matter experts; technologists; marketing experts; communications experts	Guidelines are often not formally codified but are recommended to stakeholders
Who informs?	Legal; compliance; various digital and organizational subject matter experts	Business and digital stakeholders; industry expert best practices; W3C and other technology standards and protocols	Industry best practices; organizational cultural norms

Standards Definition and Documentation

If you want your extended digital team to follow your standards, it's important to write them down. This might seem self-evident, but many organizations, when asked, are unable to produce documentation of the standards that they claim their stakeholders will not comply with. This "I'm an expert, so do what I say" dynamic is hardly fair to digital stakeholders because these stakeholders often have some digital domain expertise and are heavily impacted by the business outcomes of their online efforts (so they are informed and they have a vested interest). Here are a few things to keep in mind when documenting standards.

- **Develop a standard for documenting standards.** The first standard you should define is the structure you will use to document your standards. Having a consistent format for standards will allow your digital team to be able to access the information more efficiently and will enable you to consistently cross-reference standards. You also want to consider the platform you will use. A wiki can be a good platform for documentation. It allows for revision and version control and can be accessed by multiple standards authors. Some standards can also be integrated with various digital production systems [like a Web content management system (CMS)] so that the standards appear in the context of a workflow. For instance, there might be ready access to editorial and design standards within the context of a text editor in a CMS.

- **Determine what should be a standard.** There is almost an endless list of standards that can be defined. It's important to figure out which ones are most relevant to your organization. For instance, if your organization is getting ready to ramp up on mobile, standards related to responsive design might be important. Or, if your organization's aim is multichannel content delivery, component content authoring standards might be a priority. Sometimes organizations will place high priority on documenting standards that have caused a lot of debate, such as graphical user interface or information architecture. Let your own organizational dynamics drive the standards prioritization process.

- **Leverage what you already have.** The standards steward will also need to understand what standards your organization has already documented or where a digital standard can be largely informed by an already existing standard. Brand guidelines, style guidelines, applications development protocols, compliance mandates, and records management schedules are examples of information that might help inform or greatly impact the substance of your standards. It's important to perform an audit and detail what information exists and where it is. That way, when standards authors sit down to write standards, you'll be able to reference relevant standards easily and consistently.

Standards Dissemination

A common problem in digital teams is that they've often forgotten that their internal digital stakeholders are users as well. Typically, the experience of accessing and understanding digital standards for internal users in organizations is very low. For example, if you are a digital stakeholder trying to understand the rules of development for your organization, you are probably not interested in browsing through a beautifully designed PDF of a style guide. You just want to find the information quickly so you know, say, what font color to use for a visited link reference. The digital standards steward can help facilitate that information by being more strategic about standards dissemination.

- **Tell people about the information.** If you have established a digital community of practice (CoP) inside your organization, be sure to discuss new standards and standards revisions as they arise. Frequently, resources aren't told that a standard has changed until the standard is violated. Digital CoPs are effective because they bring together all the people in your organization who work with your digital channels. As you'll see in Chapter 8, "The Decision To Govern Well," these communities are ideal for sharing information and for training.

- **Web or Intranet-enable your standards repository.** It is essential to produce standards in Web-ready format. Often, digital standards are authored in word processing applications or published as large PDF files. Instead, organizations should make an effort to leverage the power of the hyperlink, making it easy for stakeholders and developers to click through to corresponding and related digital standards (and policy) to get the whole picture. Sometimes, there may be standards that individuals would not typically seek on their own, but might be relevant to their work at hand.

Standards Implementation

Digital standards stewards usually feel that their job is complete when they have documented the standards and placed them online. In reality, their job has just begun. The real work lies in ensuring that the standards are implemented.

- **Use tools.** When possible, an organization should use tools to implement and ensure compliance with digital standards.

If content contributors and developers must build through a narrow standards-based gate in order to get their content on the server, it's less likely that you will end up with "rogue" or non-compliant content and Web pages. You can help support the implementation of standards for visual design page structure by establishing templates in a Web content management system. For example, you can raise the quality of writing by implementing an editorial review process and workflow. If you have certain metadata tagging requirements for an online catalogue, you might implement a sophisticated auto tagging system.

This is a straight gate and narrow way, however, and not all outcomes can be achieved via tight constraints. Certain standards, particularly some editorial and design standards, need to be implemented via other means, such as employee training and education.

- **Training and education.** Not everything that is a standard can be implemented with a tool. Certain editorial concerns, for instance, might require training from internal or external experts. Many teams have found value in providing education for areas like writing for the Web or graphic design for the Web. You often won't get 100% standards compliance with training and education. People are unique, and they will interpret standards in different ways. At the end of the day, this means that you need to staff your digital team with the right people and trust them to do their job correctly.

Standards Compliance Measurement

Hopefully, if you have defined, disseminated, and implemented your standards well, compliance will be high. Still, websites and intranets are large, complex environments. Even in the best of circumstances, standards will be misunderstood or ignored in haste. That is why it is import to measure standard compliance in a consistent and automated way. You can monitor standards through spot checks and prepublication reviews, but in a large production environment, this is often a daunting task. Implementing a website auditing tool is often helpful because it allows the core digital team to provide quantified reports on things such as broken links, terminology language use, usability, compliance, and SEO. Reporting back to stakeholders about which standards they are upholding and which they are not, and creating a plan to lead the team to higher rates of compliance, is a more positive method of standards enforcement than threats that content or applications will be removed from the server.

Even after you've implemented your standards lifecycle, there will still be exceptions to the rule. There will be times when digital workers will want to break with the standards. And then each organization will have to determine when it's okay to break the rules and when it's not. These types of situation can be touchy, particularly if the resources involved in the standards breach are fairly senior in the organization (like a CEO who insists on having the picture on a homepage or wants to write lengthy, dense blog posts). In the end, these types of situations will have to be negotiated by the standards steward, authors, and the "standards breaker." During the discussion and negotiation, it is important to emphasize how the business is being put at risk due to a standards breach *and* how the business could benefit if the standards were complied with. At the end of the day, you'll never have 100% compliance, but hopefully the vast majority of your digital presence will follow the rules as defined by digital standards authors.

Identifying Standards Authors

The standards steward has a very important job, but his role would be unnecessary without the information the standards authors provided.

NOTE CHARACTERISTICS OF STANDARDS AUTHORS

The standards authors have certain characteristics:

- Have specific digital domain expertise.
- Are able to explain the rationale and context for the standard.
- Enjoy staying abreast of digital trends in their areas of expertise.

Anatomy of a Standard

Every organization will have its own way of documenting standards. But here are some components to consider when deciding on an appropriate format (see Figure 5.6).

Forms Creation Tool	➡ **Standard Title:** This area is self-explanatory.
Standard	➡ **The Standard:** Express your standards clearly and succinctly. Be sure to provide examples, code snippets, images, and anything else that will illustrate the standard and foster compliance.
InfoPath 2007 forms creation tool shall be used for forms on all Web pages that use underlying Microsoft Web technologies (e.g., IIS, Share-Point, SQL Server) and development platforms (e.g., Visual Studio .NET). Where these underlying Microsoft Web technologies are not used, a form creation tool compatible with the XForm standard will be used.	
Rationale	➡ **Rationale:** Even if people agree with a standard, they'll be more likely to comply with it if they understand why the standard has been put into place, so give the rationale for it here.
InfoPath 2007 is an XML Forms tool, included in the Enterprise License that the enterprise has with Microsoft. Using this tool allows the business to collect all responses in an underlying database structure, preferably to a network database store as a SharePoint list, a SQL Server table or relational database, or a metadata repository.	
Related Policies, Standards, and Guidelines	➡ **Related Policies, Standards, and Guidelines:** No standard lives in a vacuum. It likely has a relationship to other existing policy and standards—some Web related and others not. Listing related standards and hyperlinking to them helps create an ecosystem of standards and supports an environment where compliance is the norm.
1.15 Text-only pages 1.3 Electronic forms (accessibility) 2.1 Forms Creation Tool 2.2 Survey Tool 2.5 Portals 2.7 Website and Web page creation	
Author	➡ **Author:** This is the place to list the decision maker for the standard. When standards are published on an intranet, an email link to this "owner" is useful in case someone has a question or a request for revision.
Core Web Team	
Last Updated	➡ **Last Updated:** When was this standard last revised? Often, teams try to update the whole "book" of standards on a regular basis. This is an unrealistic and ineffective method. Individual standards have their own lifecycle. Update them when required; otherwise, leave them alone.
August 2008	

FIGURE 5.6

Forms Creation Tool standard.

When people call for governance help, the core problem—perhaps wrapped in a lot of detail about projects, workflow, personalities, decentralized management, and technology—is that resources within the organization are locked in a debate about who gets to decide the substance and content of digital standards. The resolution to this debate is simple: digital standards should be defined by those who have relevant domain expertise.

For example, design standards should be defined by staff who have expertise in areas such as typography and color. Editorial standards should be crafted by those with expertise in Web writing and content strategy. Standards related to publishing and development should be written by those who understand Web content management systems technologies *and* how best to author content so that it can be effectively moved around and delivered by those systems.

This relationship between domain expertise and standards definitions may seem self-evident, but it's often ignored inside organizations. For example, it's not unusual to find graphical design standards and norms being established by applications developers, and conversely, infrastructure technology standards being established by marketing writers with little to no digital domain expertise. And business stakeholders, who often have no skills in digital development at all, are often adamant about the supremacy of their opinions about things like information architecture, Web content management systems, and the use of social media. This phenomenon happens for a few reasons:

- **Staff assume that since they are doing the work, they have the authority to define how that work gets done.** That's usually not a valid assumption. A lot of this assumption finds its roots in the fact that the Internet and Web are relatively new platforms for business and in the early days there was a natural compression of skills in website development. The traditional webmaster *did* do everything—configure the server, make the graphics, and write the content. But today, 20 years into the commercial Web, there are resources that specialize in certain aspects of digital and often have 10–20 years honing that expertise.

- **Business stakeholders assume that because they have a vested interest in the outcomes of digital that means they should be allowed to make key decisions about how digital is deployed.** This is only somewhat true. What this really means is that they ought to be around the table when the digital strategy is being defined, rather than telling information architects that all their links need to be on the homepage.

- **Many aspects of digital touch on areas of expertise that have traditionally been the domain of the marketing communications team or a technology team, such as graphic design and infrastructure technologies, respectively.** There is an assumption of expertise or ownership because some digital disciplines have a lot of functional similarity or the skills sets are superficially similar. But just because a staff member has the expertise to select and integrate a customer relationship management system, and has been doing that for 15 years, doesn't mean that she understands Web content management systems or search engine software. And just because a writer has written marketing copy for 10 years, doesn't mean that he automatically knows how to write content in an environment where a component-based, multichannel content delivery strategy is in play. Of course, organizations should leverage the expertise of these resources while understanding that skills and methodologies likely don't transfer one-to-one to digital development.

DO'S AND DON'TS

DON'T: Assume that all the digital knowledge resides on your core team. Distributed team members can also be (and often are) serious digital domain experts. Make sure that you leverage their knowledge when getting input for developing standards.

So the history of bootstrap, make-it-up-as-you-go-along collaboration around the Web has led to a high degree of participation and ownership by many stakeholders. Because of this dynamic, core digital teams and the management that empowers them with the authority for standards authorship find themselves in the difficult position of having to rescind assumed authority for standards definition from other digital stakeholders. This is never a fun situation, although that is exactly what needs to happen in many organizations. It doesn't mean that these stakeholders cannot provide input for standards definitions—just that they have to do so within a defined set of parameters.

Finding the Experts: Input vs. Decision-Making

Over a decade ago, I worked with a large governmental organization. When I started talking about governance and decision-making, they informed me that they made decisions about standards by consensus. That meant that the entire group needed to eventually come to the same conclusion about what ought to be done online. Everyone. All agreeing to the same thing. I accepted that. It sounds good, right? It sounds nice and fair.

But as time passed and I saw the model in action, there was something that always struck me as being impractical about it. How likely is it that 40+ people (the size of their Web manager community) were going to agree about the diverse set of standards that support digital? Actually, in practice, most of the time they agreed about things. But sometimes, for key things like information architecture and infrastructure product selection, there was fierce debate. It was obvious that the whole thing would come to a head at some point, and it did. After a few years of avoiding making decisions about key standards, I watched as the organization was held back from making a good technology choice due to the disagreement of a single individual. I liked this guy. He was sharp and a strong digital domain expert.

The problem was that he was both right and wrong. He was *right* that the technology wasn't the number one choice for the particular needs of his areas of the website (although it was adequate). At the same time, he was *wrong* because the technology was the best choice for the organization as a whole. He was trying to maximize the outcome for his department's needs, not for the entire organization. In fact, it was hard for him to even see the broader perspective. But his position meant that the whole team couldn't move forward. And they didn't—for years. What a mess.

In a stroke of timeliness, I happened to be reading Peter Weill and Jeanne Ross's book on IT governance (*IT Governance: How Top Performers Manage IT Decision Rights for Superior Results*). There is a lot to take away from that book, but the thing that stood out for me and provided me with guidance was the distinction they made between providing input and making a decision. It's a distinction that seemed obvious after I read it, and it seems obvious to Web teams when I introduce the concept to them today. But I still get delighted when I watch them have an "ah ha" moment when they realize that they may have had their last standards stand-off.

So how does this apply to digital standards?

When making decisions about standards, there are two different constituencies: those with an interest and those with the authority to make the final decision. Typically, those with the authority are the people who have the following background:

- The expertise to craft a good standard.

- The authority to do so (with senior management's blessing).

I realized that this was what was missing in the room when I talked about the Web team at Cisco Systems, who were trying to make the decision about buying a Web content management system (see Chapter 1, "The Basics of Digital Governance"). No one knew who had the authority to decide the standards.

In situations like these where the authority is unclear, things generally happen:

- **Someone steps forward and assumes authority, and the group accepts the authority.** If the individual who steps forward is a domain expert and he has done his homework about the organizational and functional needs, then you might get a good outcome. If he hasn't, then you've got someone with a lot of chutzpah, but he won't necessarily lead to a good standard.

- **More than one person steps forward and assumes authority, which often creates factions.** In the instance where two people step forward, you can still have the same result: the scenario where they might be making a good or bad decision, but you also have to deal with the more likely scenario that these resources who have assumed authority probably won't agree on what the standard is. That's how the endless debate starts and never stops.

- **No one assumes authority, and the process stalls.** In this situation, the organization simply doesn't make a decision. They just have a lot of meetings talking about things, but ultimately don't move forward. In situations where there is no governance, business units or other organizational subdivisions usually just do their own thing. This is how incongruent technical and information architecture paradigms start and are sustained.

Luckily, you don't have to settle for one of these less-than-optimal situations. You can clear up standards authoring authority by completing a simple exercise.

Input and Decision-Making Exercise

Use this matrix shown in Table 5.2 to clarify digital standards decision-making. It's a simple but powerful exercise. You can create one for each standards area and for specific digital properties. List your stakeholders on the left and then tick off who will be providing input and who will be making decisions. You can use the four standards areas outlined in Chapter 1 (Design, Editorial, Publishing, and Development, as well as Network and Infrastructure). Or, if those areas are too broad or narrow, break them down or flatten them.

TABLE 5.2 INPUT AND DECISION MATRIX

Stakeholder	Input	Decision
Marketing		
Communications		
Legal		
Human Resources		
IT		
Digital		

Those people with an interest in the substance of a standard should provide input or context so that those people with expertise can effectively determine what the standards should be. This is the way to be inclusive without having to come to consensus about everything. An "interest" could mean that you are responsible for the integrity of the corporate brand, or it could mean that you are a content contributor that has to use a Web content management system on a daily basis. In many ways, providing input is like expressing requirements for standards. After those requirements are expressed, those with expertise can take the full picture into consideration and define the protocol. This input also gives the decision-maker(s) enough insight to know how to react to ever-emerging technology trends, so they know when to revise or remove ad standards or when to create new ones.

When you perform this exercise (see Table 5.3), you will see decision-making patterns arise quickly and also get a few surprises. One of them will be that the core digital team where authority for much of standards authoring often resides is often in complete agreement with their digital stakeholders. When these standards are discussed outside of the context of a pressing deadline, resources find that they all want the same thing: a high-quality effective digital presence.

TABLE 5.3 INPUT AND DECISION MATRIX FOR GRAPHICAL DESIGN STANDARDS

Stakeholder	Input	Decision
Marketing	X	X
Communications	X	
Legal		
Human Resources		
IT	X	
Core Digital Team	X	X

CONTENT GOVERNANCE

Ann Rockley, The Rockley Group

One of the primary goals of structured reusable content is the ability to create content that can be automatically published to multiple channels and dynamically adapted to customer needs and devices. To reach and maintain these goals, you need to have governance. Creating content or making changes to the structure in an arbitrary way can result in partial or full loss of automation, not to mention the loss of productivity and translation savings. Governance is critical to success!

Summary

- Standards articulate the exact nature of an organization's digital portfolio and are put into place to enable digital workers to work collaboratively and effectively in a decentralized environment.

- A standards steward is a digital generalist responsible for ensuring that all standards are written and the full lifecycle of standards compliance (definition, dissemination, implementation, and measurement) is considered.

- Standards authors are responsible for defining specific protocols for digital development. The authoring of standards is usually distributed to a number of digital domain experts.

- Organizations should have clarity regarding who provides input and who makes decisions about standards. Standards authors should gather input from organizational stakeholders, and that information should be gathered before defining standards.

Five Digital Governance Design Factors

D igital governance frameworks would be easy to design if they existed in a vacuum. But they don't. There are many pre-existing organizational factors in every business that influence which aspects of an organization ought to be accountable and responsible for making decisions about what's happening online. Sometimes the dynamics of these factors are so hard-wired into an organization's operational processes that they can be difficult to change. Staff and management feel that these dynamics are somehow ordained and immutable—"We've always worked like this." Or, more strongly, "We *must* work like this." But, in reality, almost anything in an organization *can* and *does* change, given the right forces, including its core products and services and certainly the way it governs itself.

If you look at the antecedents and history of many long-lived organizations, the strategic goals, products, services, and supporting management structures have likely changed significantly over time. Sometimes an organization's ability to transform in the face of new technologies or political and social trends is the root of its long-term strength, and in other instances, an organization's loss of core can be the beginning of its demise. This means that when organizations do change longstanding product lines or business practices, they usually do so only after serious consideration and evaluation of many factors *or* in reaction to subtle or brazenly disrupting market forces—like the Internet and the World Wide Web.

This tug of war between how organizations have worked and made decisions in the past and how they will need to work and make decisions in the information age will come to the forefront as you design your framework. There will be a dance between the existing dynamics of the organization and what digital demands at every stage of your governance framework design process—even more so once you begin the tactical work of defining strategy, policy, and standards.

Often, when organizations feel this dissonance during their digital governance design efforts, they stop. They feel that the design effort is not worth risking some organizational discomfort. In organizations whose core products and services are being disrupted by digital, failing to push through this dissonance to some conclusion is often a mistake, because they fail to thrive. If an organization is not immediately or fundamentally disrupted, then it may be able to afford to be less decisive about evaluating the impact of digital and formalizing digital governance. However, eventually, all organizations will have to have the tough conversations. Because of this, proactively addressing digital governance is much easier than being forced to do so in a reactionary mode when organizational competitive forces are compromising viability.

The Five Factors

There are five factors that regularly influence or are influenced by the digital governance framework design process. Openly considering these factors when designing your framework will help your organization remain vital and relevant, while at the same time absorbing the reality of the changes that the Web and Internet have enabled. The factors are the following:

- Corporate governance dynamics

- External demands

- Internet and World Wide Web governance

- Organizational culture

- The nature of your digital presence

How each of these factors impacts your organization will be unique. But, when undertaking the design effort, the framework design teams in all organizations will have to ask the same question: Do we change the dynamics of this design factor to suit the needs of digital, or is the substance of this dynamic so integral to the business that digital must follow its lead?

Factor 1: Corporate Governance Dynamics

Digital governance is a subset of corporate governance. So, naturally, an organization's digital governance framework will be heavily influenced by how that organization governs overall (see Table 6.1). At the most basic level, if an organization does not govern well on the whole, it's also likely that this same organization will find designing and implementing a digital governance framework difficult.

For many organizations, the digital governance framework design effort is the "tail wagging the dog" in the corporate governance arena. For instance, the framework design team may find itself challenged to determine who has decision-making authority around graphical user interface design standards in an organization that has difficulty establishing authority for corporate visual identity and brand standards. Or the team may find it impossible to establish a policy for Web records retention when their organization has no formal records management policy.

TABLE 6.1   HOW CORPORATE GOVERNANCE INFLUENCES DIGITAL GOVERNANCE

Corporate Governance		Digital Governance
The logical, legal, and fiscal structure of the organization	influences	the digital team structure and budget.
How and where organizational goals and success metrics are defined	influences	who defines digital strategy.
Which organizational entities oversee and author corporate policy	influence	digital policy stewardship and authoring.
How the organization makes decisions about shared initiatives and shared infrastructure platforms	influences	patterns for digital standards, authoring, and stewardship.

Alternately, if an organization governs well, introducing the idea of digital governance may not be as challenging. However, even when organizations have developed some governance maturity like those that function in more heavily regulated sectors such as pharmaceutical, finance, or healthcare, they may only govern certain aspects of their business well.

Within a single organization, there can be multiple governing styles of governing. And, that's okay. Businesses are systems with nodes of specialization that don't all need to be governed or managed in the same manner. Your objective is not necessarily to mimic existing organizational governing dynamics, but rather to ensure that the digital governance framework integrates well with existing governing dynamics and supports your organization's ability to do its job well—whatever that might be.

In any organization, multiyear plans, strategies, and performance measurement paradigms often align with the grid of fiscal management. For example, managers typically measure their corporate authority by the size of their budget and the number of headcount over which they have authority.

But, sometimes, digital efforts and effective governing practices cut across or run against these existing realities. For instance, the biggest (from a headcount perspective) and most profitable product line in an organization might be accustomed to basically doing whatever it likes in an organization. However, a specific dynamic, such as growing ecommerce channels, might serve to reduce that traditional authority and profitability. That can make for a tough transition for the people.

If there are aspects of your digital governance framework that require you to change the way you fund digital or don't align with the existing power hierarchy, then you should expect significant pushback. That's why, as you'll see in Chapter 7, "Getting It Done," all digital governance framework design efforts require senior leadership advocacy and sponsorship.

Factor 2: External Demands

Organizational digital systems exist in a broader ecosystem—one that extends beyond the boundaries of the organization. And that larger system often imposes requirements on an organization. Those requirements might influence who within your organization is allowed to make decisions about certain aspects of your business, including policy and standards. For digital, those demands usually fall into two categories: demands driven by the marketspace in which an organization does business and demands driven by the geographical location of where a business operates.

Market-Specific Demands

Sometimes the marketspace in which an organization does its business impacts the designation of strategy, policy, and standards decision-makers. For instance, businesses operating in the financial sector may have a legal requirement to establish a separation between certain business entities. That separation can extend to the people who are allowed access to certain information and the people who have fiduciary responsibility for various organizational subdivisions.

Superficially, this may not appear to be of concern to digital workers, but these divisions can and do impact how financial organizations cross-sell their products and services in the real world and online. Most people have experienced calling their banks to discuss their checking and credit card accounts and being transferred from division to division. While some of this behavior represents bad customer service, some of it is legally required. These same sorts of divisions can and do surface online and will impact the design of your framework, as well as your websites and supporting back-end systems.

It's important for organizations to understand, in detail, these sorts of compulsory separations. Frequently, digital workers get so focused on possibilities related to cross-channel selling that they don't stop to reflect on these deeper concerns. And, if an organization's legal department's awareness of digital is low, an organizational Web presence can unwittingly find itself out of compliance with industry-specific regulations. If these types of separations are considered and discussed in full when designing your digital governance framework, there is less chance that certain regulatory lines will be crossed in the enthusiasm of implementing new online functionality.

Geography-Related Demands

Depending on where your organization operates, regulations around the use of and access to the Internet and World Wide Web will differ. In recent years, businesses in the EU have dealt with shifting information, as it relates to the use of "cookies" and other Web browser-based tracking devices. In addition, many governmental entities have established rules about what can be viewed and sold online. For instance, in the United States, certain states prohibit the shipment of alcohol, which means that customers in those states can't buy a bottle of wine and have it shipped to their home. When considering the strategic aspects of social media organizations, your company might need to know that Facebook is blocked in China, or that LinkedIn is not an effective vehicle for employee recruitment.

DO'S AND DON'TS

DO: Remember that organizations that function globally may have more complexity in their framework—particularly when it comes to stewardship of digital policy.

Because of these dynamics and the ability to operate in many regions and nations, global businesses have to take special care in considering how policy and standards will be crafted and by whom. Their policy must be aware of and reflect national regulatory concerns, as well as regional and cultural norms. For instance, if an organization's website homepage features prominent imagery, that imagery must be appropriate for every country, and if not, the organization might need to localize that imagery (see Figure 6.1). This restriction can impact who should be designated to make certain decisions about design and editorial standards in the organization and what work gets done in the core and distributed digital team—thus, it impacts the digital governance framework.

FIGURE 6.1

The homepage for Visa in the United States and Bangladesh.

On the whole, it's important to remember that even after 20 years, digital is not a mature business space in the commercial Web. Organizations are still figuring out how to utilize digital channels effectively to their business advantage. Outside of commercial business, there is still debate and a lack of certainty regarding how existing local, national, and international laws apply to the Internet and Web, particularly as to how those laws relate to data privacy, tracking, and how much constraint an employer can put on an employee regarding the use of social media, to name a few scenarios. For this reason it's important to be strategic about the selection of your policy steward in particular because it is that person's job to keep a finger on the pulse of external regulatory concerns that may impact how your business operates online.

Factor 3: Internet and World Wide Web Governance

For digital professionals, particularly for those people who have spent their entire career in a Web-enabled business environment, it is often easy to forget that the Internet and World Wide Web are relatively new systems for business. More importantly, the actual impact of these systems is ongoing. Web and Internet policy issues are broad and deep and should be on the radar screen of your governance framework design team. It is vital to understand your organization's place and function within the evolving Internet ecosystem and be aware of significant shifts that might impact business operations and corporate and digital governance frameworks.

Digital governance is at the receiving end of a system of Internet and World Wide Web governance (see Table 6.2), so, it's important to understand which policy and standards shifts in these arenas might impact how your organization governs its digital presence.

A lot of organizations are largely disconnected from trends in Internet and World Wide Web governance, mostly because the issues being discussed, such as the debate between IPv4 and IPv6 in Internet Governance or the discussion about Open Standards and WWW governance, might not seem to be germane to everyday digital concerns of the business. That might be true for many digital practitioners, but these concerns should be on the radar of policy and standards stewards. Knowledge of these sorts of debates and their relevance to the business should be taken into consideration when designating these roles in your framework. Some other concerns worth noting are the following:

- Ecommerce taxation

- The nature and agenda of the Internet multi-stakeholder governance model

- Network neutrality

- Internet infrastructure development (physical)

- Domain name administration and management

- Personal privacy

TABLE 6.2   THE DIFFERENCES BETWEEN INTERNET, WEB, AND DIGITAL GOVERNANCE

	Scope and Issues	Interested Stakeholders
Internet Governance	The global Internet	The Internet Society (ISOC)
	Control and management of the physical Internet infrastructure	Internet Corporation for Assigned Names and Numbers ICANN)
	Control and management of domain names and numbers	Internet Governance Forum (IGF)
	Global access	Number Resource Organization (NRO)
		The United Nations (UN)
		National Governments
Web Governance	World Wide Web	The World Wide Web Consortium (W3C)
		United Nations
		National Governance
Digital Governance	Organization or enterprise	IT
	Websites	Marketing/ Communications
	Mobile sites	Legal
	Web-enabled sensors and micro-devices embedded in devices and humans	Human Resources
		Compliance

What you need to do when designing your framework:

- Designate a policy steward who has the ability to stay abreast of emerging Internet and World Wide Web policy and standards concerns.

- Ensure that both policy and standards stewards can analyze how various Internet and WWW policy and standards decisions may impact the strategic aims of the organization.

- Make sure that your organization is strategically positioned to participate in Internet and WWW-related policy debates when policy outcomes impact the vitality of your organization.

NOTE **FURTHER READING**

The Next Wave: Using Digital Technology to Further Social and Political Innovation (Brookings FOCUS Book), Darrell M. West

Networks and States: The Global Politics of Internet Governance (Information Revolution and Global Politics), Milton L. Mueller

The Global War for Internet Governance, Laura DeNardis, Yale University Press

Factor 4: Organizational Culture

Whether your organization operates in the spirit of open collaboration, highly politicized debate, top-down command and control, or a combination of these and other management styles, your organization's culture will influence your digital governance framework design efforts. That influence usually manifests itself in three significant ways:

- It may impact the process that is used to create the framework itself.

- It can influence the substance of the framework.

- It could affect how the framework is implemented.

As you'll see in Chapter 7, "Getting It Done," it's important to create an appropriate environment in which to have the tough conversations that will surely arise when you design your framework. Organizations that support a culture of collaboration might want to use a more inclusive and transparent process from start to finish when designing their digital governance framework. Alternately, organizations that have a more hierarchical, top-down decision-making culture may be able to take a more narrowly inclusive approach to framework design. Creating the framework is the first task in the digital governance implementation process. So it's important to conduct that process in a way that sets the desired tenor and tone.

Organizational culture can also impact what is possible in an organization as it relates to digital governance. A highly focused, standards definition, decision-making function with minimal stakeholder input might be the most efficient model in some situations and may even support an organization's digital strategy most effectively, but it may not marry well with an organization where the culture honors inclusive collaboration. In situations like these, the optimal framework might need to bend to suit the culture of the business, or the culture might have to change to support the new demands of digital.

In a for-profit environment, the decisive driver is often a clear one—things like fiscal viability and market-share retention. It makes little sense to maintain what has been a traditional cultural trend while at the same time leading the business's bottom line down a path to fiscal ruin (although I've watched some businesses do so). Reacting to the impact of digital, like all business disruptions, is challenging from a change management perspective. In some organizations, executives might not be equipped for the challenge. A mature business that works in a sector that is largely commoditized simply may not have the type of management and staff in place that are functionally capable of adapting to a deep disruption brought on by digital.

Even if the evolution is implemented, serious shifts in business culture due to the impact of digital may render the business unrecognizable to long-term employees. Managers will have to balance out the importance of employee retention against future business viability. Some organizations don't have the stomach for that sort of deep transformation. In already heavily impacted market segments, such as publishing, these challenges have necessarily been faced head-on with some organizations going out of business and others transforming almost beyond recognition as digital publishing pushes print publication methods and processes out of dominance (see Figure 6.2).

FIGURE 6.2
Newsweek goes out and then back into print, and *The New Yorker* puts its archive online.

Culture will also influence how your digital governance framework is implemented. Outside of an online business emergency (such as legislative activity due to questionable or illegal activity online), many organizations will implement their framework over time more quickly or more slowly, depending how the organization manages changes. But some may be able to support a more abrupt shift in governance if the organization has a history of utilizing a more rapid approach to change management.

When defining your framework, it's important to understand these cultural aspects and push to "do the right thing." That will require a degree of managerial courage, but if the disruption of digital is real, your organization's long-term health may rely on the strength of those defining your framework.

Factor 5: The Nature of Your Digital Presence

Of course, the size and range of your organization's digital presence will impact the design of your framework. In fact, in many ways, those online products and services will have a direct correlation to your digital team structure and decision-making patterns. It seems self-evident, but be sure you understand the full inventory of applications, websites, and social channels being utilized by your organization before you start your design effort. Sometimes, core digital teams try to exert control over their digital presence without really understanding the big picture of what is happening throughout the entire organization. At other times, digital team members can be so hyper-focused on the quality of one digital artifact—such as the main organizational website—that they miss other potentially high-risk digital sites and social channels that require the support of a proper digital governance framework.

DO'S AND DON'TS

DON'T: Forget that the organization's online presence is already governed by the Internet and WWW policy and standards. Stay abreast of trends in these two parent-governing systems and influence them when necessary.

A large global multinational B-to-B digital presence will necessarily have a different sort of supporting governing framework than that of a large B-to-B organization that operates in a single country or a large B-to-C company that operates its digital presence in multiple countries. Organizations with websites that carry a heavy transactional volume, like ecommerce sites, will have a different sort of governance framework than a site whose focus is largely information dissemination. And organizations that utilize social channels heavily will govern differently as well. Chapter 7 will detail how you can ensure that you understand the landscape of digital at your organization.

I've found that, overall, clear organizational governance is the exception and not the rule. Even when governing practices are clear, the dynamics and culture of an organization can mask what is going as it relates to governance. For instance, most people would think that military environments have command-and-control, top-down governance models and governing norms, but what's less intuitive is that when it comes to product design, so does Apple, Inc. In fact, in some ways, Apple delegates less accountability and decision-making authority than military organizations.

In the military, command and control is the norm except in certain specific times (like on the battle field) when soldiers are empowered to make decisions without going through the normal command and control hierarchy. So the military wears its governance framework on its sleeve, but Apple (and a lot of other organizations) wraps their governance practices up in a different cultural veneer (see Figure 6.4). If you were to examine Apple's real approach to governance overall, it might really look like a benevolent dictatorship and, in certain situations, have tighter controls than those in the military.

FIGURE 6.3
Apple iPhones—
a product of
a "benevolent
dictatorship."

Every organizational digital presence has its own DNA, but there are some common themes that organizations can consider when trying to evaluate how the nature of their digital presence might impact their framework (see Table 6.3).

TABLE 6.3   THE NATURE OF YOUR DIGITAL PRESENCE—DESIGN
            CONSIDERATIONS

Theme	Questions to Ask
Level of integration	What is the level of integration with non-digital channel strategies and processes? (If it's deep, you might want to push for the integration of digital governance with overall organizational governance now.)
Scope of your digital presence	How many websites, social channels, and mobile apps does your organization support and what is their purpose? Do they all need to be governed the same way?
Localization	Is your digital presence localized, or is everything served up in a single "international" format? Do you translate all of your content or just some of your content? Who in your organization does the translation? Who does the review?
Rate of change	Do you update content every minute, hour, daily, or only once a month? How often do you deploy new applications and content?
Content and systems architecture	How many content publishing systems exist in your digital environment? Who pays for them? How do they intersect with other systems and content on your servers? How is your core digital hardware and software infrastructure architected and administered?
Mission criticality	Is your digital presence mission-critical to the business?

Don't Give Up

The consideration of all of these factors (and others unique to your organization) creates a complex design challenge, which is why a lot of organizations put off designing and implementing a governance framework until the situation absolutely demands it—such as when a website needs a new information architecture or technical platform and the core digital team realizes that they don't have the authority to effect that change, or when the risk of continuing to operate in an ungoverned manner becomes too great. In those situations, though, it's unlikely that organizations can take the time to make the right choices. So it's important to be proactive about designing your framework in advance. Doing it at a time when the organization can take the time to do the job well is important. The next chapter explains how to get this framework accomplished and in place.

Summary

- The nature of your digital governance framework will be impacted by five key design factors.

- Corporate governance dynamics will impact your digital governance framework because digital governance is a subset of corporate governance and will therefore inherit dynamics from its parent.

- Market-specific and geography-specific regulatory musts and constraints will impact your framework design, as will social norms in regions, nations, and locales.

- Internet and World Wide Web governance are the cornerstones of digital governance, and trends in both of these domains will impact, sometimes substantively, how organizations must govern digital.

- An organization's culture will influence how an organization designs its digital governance framework, what the substance of the framework is, and how it is implemented.

- The nature of your digital presence will drive the design of your digital governance framework, especially the structure, roles, and responsibilities of your digital team.

CHAPTER 7

Getting It Done

The governance framework design effort is a good opportunity for your organization's digital stakeholders to learn how to work and collaborate better. So, even if you already have a sense of who on your digital team ought to have the authority to make decisions related to digital strategy, policy, and standards, it's still important to go through the design effort with a larger team. Because it's not just the end state that is important, but rather the interim conversation, collaboration, and compromise required to build your framework. Those activities will bring your team into better communication, better community, and better alignment.

Most importantly, in environments where effective digital governance practices haven't been implemented, the de facto core digital team is often in an uncomfortable position. In many cases, they are struggling to produce a functioning digital presence in a chaotic development environment, with no real authority to define and enforce standards. These teams are hungry for authority, tired, frustrated, and feel (and often are) underappreciated. That's not the best dynamic for defining governance practice. So, even if you are a key stakeholder with a lot of institutional knowledge and digital domain expertise, it's important to remember that creating a digital governance framework is not an opportunity to create another functional, decision-making silo. Instead, take the time to do the job right. It will be well worth the effort.

There are four main aspects to consider when creating the digital design framework:

- Identifying a sponsor and an advocate.

- Populating the design team.

- Starting the design effort.

- Implementing the framework.

Identifying a Sponsor and an Advocate

There are a lot of unique organizational nuances to digital governance, but one common theme is that, without a sponsor or an advocate, digital governance frameworks are often defined but seldom implemented. So, if you are not in a capacity to implement your framework through your own authority, make sure that you seek alignment with someone in your organization who does have the capacity to recommend or implement the sometimes substantive changes that can occur when digital governance frameworks are put into action (see Figure 7.1).

FIGURE 7.1
Pick someone to lead the team.

The advocacy role can sometimes be a tough role to fill. As you'll learn in Chapter 8, "The Decision To Govern Well," sometimes leadership isn't really eager to establish formal digital governance. Often, they can't see, don't understand, or in some extreme circumstances, aren't even open to hearing about the benefits and risk-mitigating dynamics of proper digital governance. Even in these extreme circumstances, every digital governance success story—the ones with the happy ending of a well-funded, well-formed, properly empowered digital team—includes the existence of an executive advocate. Sometimes the advocate takes a heavy interest and participates in the governance framework formation. At other times, the advocate simply writes the memo that announces the framework. Either of these levels of participations (and anything in between) can be effective if your advocate is well-selected because often just the basic imprimatur of a person "in charge" is all that is needed to get your framework implementation started and completed.

Organization: Description of Scope:	Core							
STRATEGY								
Digital Governance Sponsorship and Advocacy								

FIGURE 7.2

Digital governance framework sponsorship and advocacy.

So, let's consider the only line on your framework grid that is likely left blank: "Governance Sponsorship and Advocacy" (see Figure 7.2). At this juncture, consider who in your organization has the authority to make the changes required to support your new digital governance framework. It might be an individual, an executive, or maybe a senior management committee. Who the advocate is will vary greatly from organization to organization, but usually the resource is very senior.

Depending on the sector in which an organization operates, there are certain trends that become evident surrounding the person who becomes an advocate and sponsor (see Table 7.1). Often, this selection stems from how revenue is driven into the organization, or it's based on legacy (pre-digital) roles in the organization, or what part of the organization already has control of or drives digital.

Your digital governance advocate's first task will be to form the digital governance framework design team.

Dispersed Core			Distributed			Ad Hoc	Extended						

TABLE 7.1 TYPICAL DIGITAL GOVERNANCE ADVOCATES

Type of Organization	Possible Advocates
B-to-B	Chief Marketing Officer (CMO)
	Chief Information Officer (CIO)
	Chief Operating Officer (COO)
	Head of Communications
B-to-C	Chief Executive Officer
	CMO
	CIO
	Head of Communications
	Head of Product Development
Government	CIO
	Public Affairs
	Head of Communications
	General Council
Higher Education	Office of the President
	Vice-Chancellor's Office
	Head of Admissions
	Registrar
Non-Profit	Head of Development
	Executive Team
	Head of Membership
	Marketing Communications

One of the most effective things an organization can do is to co-locate its complete core digital team to report to a single manager. But housing writers in IT or graphical application developers in marketing feels really wrong to some organizations—often because the senior management doesn't have the knowledge to manage or direct these resources. However, you have to ask yourself 20 years into the Web, is that a good reason to compromise the quality of digital?

The complete rift between these two teams might have made more sense when IT was building client-server applications for its internal customers, and there were years between client interface updates. But to support an ever-changing dynamic digital presence, organizations should consider that it might be time to bring these teams closer together. Shouldn't organizations demand broader competence from their chief marketing and chief information officers? Or is digital important enough in your organization that you need a stand-alone digital team led by a very senior manager—perhaps a peer of the chief marketing or chief information officer? All those models are viable, but trying to shoehorn digital into the narrowness of pre-Web organizational structures will probably not lead to the best outcome.

Populating the Design Team

Don't underestimate the value and effect of a properly sponsored and formed design team. The governance design team often becomes a powerful entity within an organization. In many instances, the framework design team will transform itself into the digital strategy team. So it's important to get the leadership and membership right. Beware of self-selected digital governance design teams populated with only core digital team stakeholders, because they are likely to be seen as self-serving and their efforts, however sound, are often largely disregarded.

Team Leadership

You'll probably find that getting the design effort off the ground is the most difficult task. While your digital governance sponsor and advocate will be an essential voice for the initial call to action for the organization and for approving and emplacing the final framework, it is unlikely that such a high-level resource will have the time (or tactical expertise) to lead the design effort. Usually, digital governance efforts have been effectively led by core Web team leads, marketing officers, COOs, and CIOs. But there's no definitive answer here. It's not so much about the title as it is about ensuring that those who lead the design effort have a broad and balanced perspective regarding the full range of digital properties being governed. Consequently, that means that resources who work in a particular silo of the organization and have a narrow interest or agenda might not be a good pick.

DO'S AND DON'TS

DO: Get executive sponsorship for your digital governance framework efforts. While you can define roles and responsibilities for digital, usually, you can't give yourself authority over others in your organization without the support of your executive team.

Sometimes, the head of the de facto core digital team self-selects as the leader of the design team. That can be a strong choice, but sometimes this leader is not the most open-minded. Often, the core digital team lead has an ax grind when it comes to digital standards being upheld, and it might see the governance design effort as an opportunity to focus power. In situations where there is a lot of contention and debate between the core digital team and other organizational stakeholders, designating the core team leader can appear to be more of a declaration of war than the olive branch that the organization needs to foster more positive collaboration.

So, be careful in these sorts of situations. If this resource does end up leading the design team, make an extra effort to create an environment where all voices can be heard. On paper, the outcome might be the same (a lot of decision making regarding standards in the core Web team), but the process used to reach the outcome can be the difference between a fun collaborative work environment and one where the work dynamic take a passive aggressive tone.

Do You Need Outside Support, or Can You Do It Alone?

Your organization can develop its own digital governance framework without outside support, but it's not a side job. You need to dedicate resource time to it, just as you would a website redesign or technology replatform. So, if you don't have time to do your framework properly, you might need support outside of your team and leadership. That support can be simple administrative support, such as organizing meetings, taking minutes, and following up with members on action items. Or you might need a facilitator to help drive the process forward and keep the team on track.

If you do use a facilitator, be sure that the person you choose is knowledgeable about digital and can be objective about the dynamics of the organization. Sometimes, you can find a facilitator from the administrative side of your organization, while other times you'll need to use an external resource. You might also need to seek additional support if the following conditions occur:

- Your organization has a lot of dysfunction or a contentious dynamic has developed around digital development.

- Your business is forced into assembling a large digital governance design team due to organizational dynamics.

- Attempts to establish a digital governance framework have failed repeatedly.

Team Membership

Your design team must be able to have meaningful and fluid conversation in real time. That means that people who can answer important questions such as: "Can we move the digital team from marketing to IT?" or "Can we change the way we budget for digital?" need to be in the room while you are designing. If you have to leave the room and follow up with managers to get context around and answers to these sorts of questions, your team is not properly resourced. Likewise, if no one in the room can speak strategically to information and technical architectures, user experience, content strategy, and digital analytics, your team is not properly resourced.

Sometimes, an organization might have an existing team in place that can be leveraged to support the governance design effort. If that is the case, as a best practice, try leveraging that team first before forming a new one. The result you are looking for is a governance framework—not the establishment of a redundant administrative or working group.

To foster real-time conversation, you won't want a large group. But, at the same time, you want to make sure that no aspect of your organization is excluded in the design process. And, as with your strategy definition team, you have to strike a balance between digital domain expertise and organizational expertise. For a lot of organizations, forming a small team that meets all of these criteria is a challenge. In principal, a team sponsored by one or two leadership figures (like the CIO or CMO) and populated by the core digital team lead(s) and strategic digital business stakeholders (like regional Web managers or brand or business line Web managers) is a good place to start. From there, you might want to add non-obvious members, like those from your legal department or operations. But, already, if you include all of these resources, your design team might be getting too large to be effective.

A productive tactic is to form a working group aligned with an already existing cross-functional executive team that represents the organization in full. The working group can be tasked to define the framework and carry it back to the senior group for codification. This less inclusive process is most effective if the group chartering the working group has broad perspective over the organization and is willing to make sure that all key digital stakeholders are able to provide input and voice their concerns (much like the inputs and decisions exercise you use when establishing standards).

Once your framework design team leadership and membership is established, your advocate can announce the digital governance framework initiative and the team's mission and agenda, and the governance framework design effort can begin in earnest.

Starting the Design Effort

You have an advocate and a sponsor, a design team has been formed, and the governance initiative has been announced to the organization. Now, you are ready to start your design effort in earnest. How do you get the work done? Because the results of the lack of digital governance are broad, deep, and pervasive (and usually uncomfortable), it's easy to believe that coming up with the solution will take a lot of effort over an extended period of time and be just as disconcerting. That doesn't have to be the case. If your framework design team is inclusive and the design effort is done with a spirit of collaboration, designing a framework can be a relatively simple task. There are a few measures you can put in place to ensure that happens.

Understand Your Digital Landscape

Sometimes, organizations are in such disarray digitally that they really don't understand the fundamental landscape of their digital presence. Before you get started assigning accountability and authority, you'll need to pursue a level of information gathering and analysis. For instance, you'll need to gather and understand information like the following:

- Organizational structure and reporting chains
- Inventory of website domains, mobiles applications, and social software accounts
- Content inventories and Web page editorial responsibilities
- Any documented digital policy
- Any documented digital standards
- Style guides and best practices
- Digital analytics to understand online usage patterns
- Online survey results, usability study results, and so on

Don't worry! Most digital teams don't have this information at their fingertips. So it's important to retrieve the information before you start, because having this sort of information at hand will help your team answer fundamental questions while designing the framework. Usually, the framework design team can create a working group to gather this information and provide it to the team. Most likely, the head of the core digital team will play a large role in this information gathering process, but be sure to include other stakeholders in this process. It's a better scenario for the team to retrieve more information than they need and discard it during the design process rather than to find out after you've created a design that it does not take into account all of the use cases for digital in your organization.

DON'T: Forget to consider the scope of your framework before you get started. Sometimes teams can be hyper-focused on governing one aspect of an organization's online presence, like websites, while ignoring others, like social channels.

How Long Will It Take?

A digital governance framework design effort can take as little or as much time as you'd like. The decision is yours. Usually, the amount of time an organization chooses to take with its design effort has a lot to do with how critical the effort is. If your design effort is taking place in the wake of some online mess, such as improper content, security breaches, or other negative attention, then it can be fast. If there is no real drive to get it done, then it can end up being a long, drawn-out process. It's your organization's decision. Organizations that are serious about governing well move quickly—organizations that aren't as serious, less so. Those statements have shown themselves to be true in organizations large and small, so size doesn't matter. You can get it done quickly if you're serious.

That said, digital governance frameworks are not complicated, but the office politics behind them can be. If you work in a highly politicized organization, working through the organizational dynamics can add a lot of time to your effort. A well-formed design team with strong leadership can help minimize side debates about authority and power. But, if there has been a lot of disagreement about the digital presence and who has authority to make decisions, some of that debate will spill over into the design process. So plan accordingly.

Table 7.2 should help you understand the basic activities in the design effort and give you a sense of how long these activities will take. Use this as a guide, not a rule. Every organization is different. Some businesses make decisions slowly and others more quickly. For example, it's possible for a massive global corporation to make all the decisions in the table during a single two-day offsite, or a small non-profit might deliberate over the same set of decisions over the course of a year.

TABLE 7.2 GOVERNANCE TASKS AND TIME COMMITMENT

Task	Description	Time Commitment
Information gathering and preparation	Gather digital presence and digital human resource demographic information; organize and project-manage the digital governance framework design effort.	Norm: 1 month to 1 business quarter Consideration: Most businesses will be able to gather this information in a month or two. For large global multinationals that are fairly well organized, it might take you up to one business quarter, and you may require a dedicated resource or outside support. If you are a large global multinational organization and your digital human infrastructure and digital online presence are in disarray, this may take more time.
Define digital team structure	Define the core, distributed, and extended Web teams and any working groups and steering committees.	Norm: 1-3 business days Consideration: Could take potentially up to a week when the organization is complex or in a diversified management structure.
Identify digital strategy, accountability, and authority	Discuss and identify accountability and decision-making authority for digital strategy.	1 half-day working session
Identify digital policy, stewardship, and authorship	Discuss and identify policy steward and policy authors.	1 half-day working sessions
Digital standards stewardship	Identify who should be responsible for managing the standards lifecycle.	1 half-day working session
Digital standards, authorship input, and decision exercise	Determine who provides input for and who makes the final decision for digital standards.	2 half-day working sessions Considerations: This can take up to three business days for very large and complex organizations.

Typically, teams that get the best results are the ones that commit concentrated time to the effort. In reality, designing the framework is often the first constructive cross-organizational collaboration that members of the digital team have been engaged in. A lot of important conversations that perhaps should have happened over the years often do happen in these design meetings, so the best results won't be achieved as effectively in a series of short hour-long meetings scattered over several months. Ideally, a two-day offsite is the most effective way of developing a framework—or at least for getting most of the way there. If that's not going to happen in your organization, try to create the same intensity in your office or at least in a series of half-day meetings that happen not less than a week apart.

Many organizations feel that they have deep governance concerns when in reality they simply haven't taken the time to sit down and talk things through. Or, if they do sit down and talk about them, it's in the middle of a project where there are timelines and other pressing concerns that can skew perspectives. A happy occurrence is that often teams find out during their design process that they are in deep alignment regarding digital governance practices—once they actually sit down and talk about it outside of the context of projects and deadlines. Your digital governance frameworks will become the foundation of your digital operations. Make the time to do your best work.

At Last—Implementing the Framework

Your design team has done its job, and you have an agreed-upon framework for digital authority and decision making in your organization. Congratulations! But this is just the beginning. Now you need to implement your design. And, even more so than the design itself, the implementation will be highly specific to your organization.

Remember that your framework design document is a schematic of how things ought to work. It takes people to move the schematic from theory into practice. At this point, it's important not to lose momentum from the design phase of governance to the implementation phase. It's a fact that too many governance framework design efforts never take hold simply because they were never implemented. Perhaps the team putting the design together felt that the existence of a framework document somehow made it a reality. Or sometimes the governance team didn't have the authority or resources to implement the changes they had devised. These types of challenges can be mitigated with proper sponsorship.

DO: Remember that the implementation of your digital governance framework begins with the process that you use to define it. Make sure that your process is one that resonates with digital stakeholders in your organization.

DON'T: Try to assert authority over digital stakeholders and colleagues during the framework-design process—keep it collaborative.

If the changes from your de facto governance model to your formal model are minimal, the tactics of the implementation can be simple. But if the changes are deeper, you may need to develop a formal implantation plan and enlist the help from those with expertise in organizational change management. However, be forewarned— because this is a slightly simplistic view, a small organizational change can cause a big reaction among staff members. For instance, those who work in digital have assumed authority for aspects of digital, and sometimes after the framework design process, they find that they no longer have the same authority. Perhaps the resources that do get authority and accountability for certain aspects of digital find that they aren't interested in having authority over these areas. Again, this is why it's important to have a well-formed design team and to consider the following when implementing your framework.

- **Formally emplace the framework.** If you've selected your framework sponsor well, this resource should be at a senior enough level of the organization to formally initiate the implementation of any changes in position or authority that your framework recommends. Make sure that happens. A document doesn't make a change. In the simplest case, a communication to relevant parties can suffice. In more sophisticated cases, job descriptions may need to be rewritten, budgetary authority for certain aspects of digital shifted, or perhaps a new digital division created. In some cases when the changes in management accountability and roles are truly significant, a formal change-management strategy might need to be defined and implemented. Sometimes, digital team members (used to a fast-paced, agile work environment) don't fully appreciate the effort required in changing the work dynamics of a large organization. Sometimes, governance shifts can take a year or more to implement.

- **Communicate.** One of the biggest differentiators between organizations that succeed in improving their digital governance practices and those that don't is how effectively they communicate the new framework to the organization. The framework design document is not the end point but a way station in the process of implementing formal governance. In most frameworks, there will be newly established working groups and communities of practice set into place to make decisions about digital and to communicate those decisions to the larger organization—or, in some cases, to help inform key digital stakeholders regarding best practices.

- **Make a distinction between digital production and digital governance.** Your digital governance framework is just that—a framework for decision making. It should not be applied to day-to-day production. For instance, just because your core digital team might be responsible for establishing editorial standards doesn't mean that they have to approve every piece of content that goes on the site. It means that the standards author is responsible for defining the substance of the editorial standard and helping to support an environment where those standards are easy to uphold. Don't confuse the two. You might develop more tactical levels of governance, like content governance or taxonomy governance, but those are different, more production-focused activities than what have been described in this book.

BRAIN TRAFFIC—DIGITAL GOVERNANCE AND CONTENT

Kristina Halvorson

If we're going to treat our "information assets" as such, we need to create and publish digital content as though it were a disposable commodity. There's a reason we talk about content going "live"—once it's out there, if we don't take care of it, it will die on the vine. Redundant, outdated, trivial, irrelevant, off-brand, inaccurate ... there are a million ways content can go bad. When we establish and practice true governance, we build a common framework for content management across silos that give us guardrails and guidelines for maintaining our content's integrity over time and across platforms.

Summary

- There are four aspects to consider when creating your digital governance framework. They are identifying a sponsor and advocate; populating the design team; overseeing the design effort; and implementing the framework.

- Identifying a sponsor and advocate for your design effort is crucial. The advocate will ensure that the framework can be implemented in the organization. Sometimes it's difficult to find a leader to fill this role because leadership can be relatively disconnected from digital, particularly when the relationship of digital to the bottom line is not straightforward.

- The digital governance framework design team should be led by a resource who is able to maintain objectivity regarding the roles and responsibilities for digital. The framework design team itself should be inclusive. The design team lead should ensure that all aspects of the organization are represented on the team or that all aspects of the organization are consulted during the design process.

- The design phase has six aspects: information gathering and preparation; defining the digital team; identifying digital strategy, accountability, and authority; identifying digital policy stewardship and authorship; determining digital standards stewardship; and conducting standards inputs and decisions exercises.

- It is important to formally emplace your framework after it has been designed. That includes formally implementing the framework, as well as making sure the substance of the framework is effectively communicated to all relevant stakeholders in your organization. It is important to be clear that a digital governance framework is not a production model. Standard operating procedures and workflow processes may still need to be developed to support day-to-day digital production.

CHAPTER 8

The Decision To Govern Well

Clearly defined or not, there will always be governing dynamics when a group of people come together to achieve a common goal. However, whether or not an organization governs *well* is a matter of choice. For organizations that do choose to govern their digital presence well, the rewards can be great, not only for the organization but also for its students, members, customers, or citizens—whoever is interacting with them online. But all too often, organizations of all types choose to ignore the call for sound governance, even when the state of their digital presence or the organizational risk created by a suboptimal digital presence all but demands that governance concerns be addressed. There are a variety of reasons why this laissez-faire attitude exists.

Some of the most frequently heard reasons for *not* establishing an effective digital governance might sound familiar:

- The diversity of product offerings of a global multinational organization. ("We're soooo decentralized" or "Every business unit is *very, very* different. We can't work the same way.")

- The intellectual autonomy and stubbornness of a highly educated staff at a university or researched-focused organization. ("Those PhD professors just won't listen!")

- The consensus decision-making style of a large non-profit or governmental organization. ("We don't govern anything" or "We're not *for* profit. That changes everything.")

None of the above dynamics are unique. On the whole, all three of these dynamics exist in every organization I've ever worked with— at varying levels; however, none of them are reasons to choose *not* to govern well. Instead, they are reasons to choose to govern *better*.

Governing takes work and effort and compromise. Even in organizations where one would think governance would be a no-brainer, like the military, people still have trouble governing their digital presence. That's because very seldom are those previously stated concerns the real reasons why digital governance has not taken hold. They are just the easy-to-speak-of ones. The real reasons are often much simpler.

Reason One: The Transformation Is Too Hard

Most people will try just about anything to get around a problem before they change the way they work from day to day. I've seen business processes that simply made no sense at all, but were in place simply to help preserve legacy work practices. A classic is the marketing team that still produces a print-focused brochure that is never printed and physically distributed, but rendered as a PDF and put online for customers and prospects to read. Why? Because their employees' jobs are defined and shaped around that process. Or, put more simply, because the organization has always done it that way.

For organizations whose business model was established prior to the advent of the World Wide Web, deciding to change tried-and-true organizational decision-making and accountability norms can be highly political or destabilizing to human resources. As mentioned earlier, certain processes or standards for working may appear to be immutable when, in reality, there are other ways to work. Also, understandably, a lot of people derive a sense of personal power from their position in a management structure, the amount of budget they control, or the degree of authority and negotiating power they have with their peers. All of these things can lead to a gridlock when it comes time to implement a new framework.

Defining a digital governance framework is relatively simple compared to *implementing* it. Some digital teams see that dilemma coming before they even get started, so they just don't get started in the first place. That's unfortunate because, likely, these teams could benefit most from a formalized and well-implemented digital governance process.

For the lucky few, a newly defined governing framework will simply solidify the good digital governing and development practices of an already well-formed digital team. But for most, the framework will represent a (sometimes radical) shift from business as usual. If your framework falls in the radical shift digital disruption camp, then your digital governance efforts might stall after your definition phase. In these situations, sometimes the core team would rather struggle through the pain they know (not enough budget, no executive sponsorship, and an inability to negotiate standards with their digital stakeholders) than venture out into the unknown terrain of digital governance.

Reason Two: We're Too Important to Fail

Sometimes organizations choose not to improve digital governance because they feel too important to fail. In these situations, there is often organizational hubris where organizational leadership feels that their legacy market position or some other level of clout leaves them impervious to the impact of digital—even in the face of real indicators that the organization might be at real risk. Let's call this the "Blockbuster Syndrome" (see sidebar). But this isn't just a for-profit stance. I've seen this attitude in higher education in instances where elite universities didn't feel there was a need to improve online student services or consider embracing new trends in online education. This "we can't fail" attitude can also exist in governmental organizations or non-governmental organizations where adequate funding is almost guaranteed year after year.

In the non-profit sector, there is a combination of these dynamics. Some non-profits or not-for-profit entities have a powerful brand that is distinct from their mission. That identity, coupled with a large endowment and donor pool, can leave these organizations feeling very comfortable, and their leadership feeling as if they can operate by a different set of rules when it comes to digital.

The risk of this sleepy posture is that a complete disregard for governance concerns means that the organization will not be aware when the ground shifts underneath it. In particular, if organizations wholly disregard the digital strategy aspect of governance and fail to make a real connection between digital performance and the overall organizational goals (even when those connections are obvious), they can find themselves ill-prepared to make the maneuvers required to stay relevant or profitable when, seemingly, all of a sudden, the digital disruptions hit their marketspace.

The Blockbuster Syndrome

Sometimes organizations miss the target when it some to digital. I'm not talking about the type or targeting that leads to low user experience or a bad website design. I'm talking about missing the target to the extent that your company goes out of business. While a lot of businesses have been impacted by digital and struggle to come up with an appropriate market response, some seem overly reticent to what many perceive to be an obvious market disruption.

An example of this was Blockbuster's response (or lack of response) to shifts in the distribution model for at-home entertainment. It took the better part of a decade for Redbox and Netflix to gain market share over Blockbuster. How do companies that "own" a market sector fail so grandly? Factors that come into play in the Blockbuster Syndrome are the following:

A digitally conservative leadership. This might include the executive level and, in some cases, a board of directors that is completely tone-deaf to the market disruption.

A healthy cash reserve. Businesses that are rich in cash often have a lot of room for error—too much room sometimes. That cash comfort affords an organization the luxury of watching a market trend for a while (too long) before reacting.

Underestimating the transformation. A lot of mature businesses underestimate the depth of the digital transformation and the amount of time it will take for a large business to integrate the dynamics of digital with the rest of the business. Digital start-ups can work agilely naturally—because they are small. Mature businesses have to work at being agile—and then make the transformation.

After a digital conservative leadership with a healthy cash reserve finally figures out that their business is in trouble, it's often too late for them to make the changes required to remain competitive.

Reason Three: We're Too Profitable to Fail

In an environment where profit is adequate to satisfy executives and shareholders, there is often little incentive to improve anything because the business is profitable *enough*. Why rock the boat when the sea is calm? Not unlike organizations that see themselves as too important to fail, some businesses see the immediate integrity of the balance sheet as an indicator that digital has not yet hit their market sector. Or, more strongly, that digital may be irrelevant to their marketspace.

I often have conversations with digital workers who state that there are executives in their organization who are still skeptical about the value of digital for anything more than creating digital brochure-wear. To the executive's defense, it is true that digital has disrupted different vertical markets in different ways and at different paces, but complete inattention to digital governance and performance is a mistake. The disruption of digital is too broad, deep, and complex to be disregarded on the whole. Depending on the reality of digital disruption, the stance of being largely bulletproof to digital disruption might be spot-on, or more likely, it might be management hubris that will lead to the downfall of your business.

Even *if* your organization might be bulletproof to digital disruption at the moment, at the very least, any organization needs to govern digital well enough so that it is in compliance with regulatory concerns and able to uphold the integrity of the brand online through the implementation and support of basic quality standards. From a more strategic perspective, every organization has a responsibility to monitor the impact of digital on its market so that it is poised to be more proactive about digital development if and when market impact begins to show itself in substantive ways.

Reason Four: Difficult People

Occasionally, staff in an organization doesn't want to point to governance problems because the cause of the governance problem includes a powerful or influential business unit. The power of the group or individual can be derived from a variety of sources, including their ability to deliver revenue to the company's bottom line, their social or business proximity to a key executive, or their tenure and legacy organizational knowledge. Digital workers are sometimes reluctant to run counter to these resources. So, instead of pointing out how a particular digital stakeholder's behavior is impacting the business in a negative way, they remain silent in order to remain non-confrontational (or in some instances to keep their jobs).

It takes a substantive amount of managerial courage to manage through a negative organizational management gauntlet. As I mentioned in Chapter 2, "Your Digital Team: Where They Are and What They Do," often digital workers aren't offered the same sorts of managerial development opportunities as other employees, so sometimes they just don't know how to deal with powerful and contentious managers and individual contributors. Even when digital workers are equipped with appropriate negotiation skills, it can still be a tough battle. I've heard many stories of digital workers going to management with solid metrics and evidenced-based stories of digital failure, risk, and opportunity and being all but ignored by senior and executive level managers. In a few rare instances, the digital workers have even been penalized for stepping "out of bounds."

How much vocational risk a worker wants to assume is a matter of personal choice. But sometimes these "politics" can be so strong that any efforts at formalizing digital governance or otherwise maturing digital can be very challenging. This is a tough situation for employees by all measures, but it's important to understand the dynamic and to recognize it for what it is. Once identified, these human resource-related concerns really aren't as complex as they appear, and a solution can be crafted. But sometimes the situations can be very challenging, and given the existing dynamics, a digital worker might decide that it's not worth taking the vocational risk and that, in extreme cases, in order to continue growing a career, that person might need to move on to another organization.

DO'S AND DON'TS

DO: Remember that any organization can be unexpectedly impacted by digital disruption. Digital executives need to be vigilant and prepared to address that impact when it occurs.

Moving Forward in Less Than Ideal Circumstances

On the whole, the less-than-optimal dynamics described earlier contribute to the deep frustration of many digital workers. Not just because it denies them their rightful place at the governance table, but because it minimizes digital workers' expertise and often relegates their role to one of a production-focused Web page "putter-upper." It ignores the reality that frequently digital workers are the first people to see new ways for their organization to leverage the Internet and Web. Because digital workers have a forward viewpoint on an emerging market technology space, digital workers are often the first to understand where the organization's market share or brand is eroding due to low digital quality, and they are the first to see where there might be an opportunity to innovate and create with a competitive advantage.

Personally, I sometimes find it frustrating to work with digital teams in organizations where that expertise is being stifled due to a lack of clarity around digital governance. It seems like a tremendous waste of organizational knowledge. In reality, many digital workers are eager to share their knowledge and contribute in a substantive way to the organization's bottom line—if only they were given the chance. So, given this reality, how does a digital worker help an organization move forward with digital governance? Let's take a look.

In situations where organizations do *not* see the value in formally governing digital, there are a few tactics that can work to break through the gridlock and jump-start a digital governance effort— or allow you to more effectively manage digital while you're working on the governance model. They are as follows:

- Aligning internal digital resources
- Quantifying the risk of a low-quality "ungoverned" digital presence
- Quantifying and promoting the upside of digital

All of these tactics should be prominent in the context of a formalized digital governance framework, but they are not a complete replacement for a well-implemented digital governance framework. However, if you're faced with a situation where you are unable to illicit sponsorship from executives, these tactics can help mitigate some of the operational risks associated with immature digital governance. And these tactics will often point the organization in the right direction, as some of these behaviors can illuminate the value of digital governance to the organization.

Internal Alignment

It is good to see three different levels of alignment around digital in an organization: one at the senior management or executive level, one at the middle management level, and one at the practitioner level. In large organizations, that alignment can effectively fall into these groups:

- **Executive:** Digital steering committee

- **Core digital team:** Center of excellence

- **Digital practitioners:** Community of practice

Your organizational may not choose to use these names, but here is a description of the functions they serve.

Digital Steering Committee

This team is responsible for establishing digital strategy and ensuring that what happens online is in harmony with the company's business objectives. In the formal framework, these people would be your digital strategy decision-makers. In the absence of a formal digital governance framework, it's still possible to bring senior resources together to help steer the general direction of digital. If you are junior to these resources, pulling this team together might be a challenge. An effective tactic in this instance might be to propose the inclusion of the digital strategy agenda to an already existing cross-functional management committee or working group—such as an executive team or a global MarCom strategic group. Effective results can be achieved by introducing a digital agenda to these sorts of teams on a quarterly basis.

If your senior digital team members are fortunate enough to engage leaders at this level, make sure that when you've got your moment on their agenda you focus on how better digital governance and online quality can add value to the business by enhancing revenue and mitigating risks. Sometimes when digital workers get the opportunity to speak with senior leaders, they flounder by discussing the tactics of a technology selection, content strategy, or the like. That work *is important*, but it does not need to be discussed at this executive level. Executives assume that their employees (and that includes digital workers) know how to get their work done. What they need to know from senior digital team members is how they should enable digital efforts through the commitment of fiscal or human resources. But before they make that commitment, they are going to want to hear a business case, not a talk on digital best practices. Engaging executives in this way often makes the case for a more formal effort in digital governance, especially when the opportunity and risk aspects of improving digital are emphasized.

Digital Center of Excellence

A digital center of excellence can be established, absent a formal digital governance framework. The center of excellence is a hub populated by domain experts who can inform standards and advise other organizational practitioners. They also align digital with the rest of the business so that they can inform management about the business value of a more orchestrated approach to digital governance. In many instances, effective core digital teams are able to boost their profile and authority by honing their expertise and "upping their game" in the organization and informally stepping into this role. In this manner, the core digital team can become the de facto digital leads in an organization.

Naturally, this course has its limitations. Those people outside of the center of excellence can still refuse to comply with best practices as outlined by this team. But 80 percent compliance to an established set of best practices is better than no common core of best practices and guidelines. When the core team sharpens its leadership skills, models best practices, and learns to speak the language of business, usually the team will find that executives who had not considered digital to be a strategic asset for the business in the past will have a change of heart now.

Digital Community of Practice

Establishing a digital community of practice inside the organization is an effective way to align all the tactical resources working on your digital presence. A community of practice is a collaborative forum with open membership. The agenda of a digital community of practice varies, but often it is leveraged to do the following:

- Pilot various digital initiatives, which substantively demonstrate a more orchestrated approach to digital development.

- Establish a forum in which to discuss and come into alignment around differences related to policy, standards, and guidelines.

- Provide an environment for training digital resources on new technologies and digital practices.

- Keep digital resources connected and in basic collaboration while an organization seeks to establish a more formal governance framework.

The digital core team plays a key role in the establishment of communities of practice. But, in this informal community, it should be careful not to adopt an attitude of "do what I say," but instead to create an environment where everyone's opinions are heard, and true discussion and open debate can happen. These grassroots communities, when well run, can begin to align a global digital team that is out of sync.

DO'S AND DON'TS

DON'T: Forget that digital governance framework implementation involves realigning human resources—that's different than redesigning user interfaces or implementing a technology stack. It's harder and less predictable.

Also, alignment at the grassroots level is an effective way to demonstrate to senior leadership the power behind the unified approach to digital. While more junior resources in the organizations may not be able to give themselves the authority to move or increase the digital budget and head count in an organization, they can certainly begin to come to consensus around digital quality guidelines and present a unified front to management. There is nothing more powerful than a well-organized, good functioning cross-functional team going to executives with a unified supported request for resources. That request could be for technology, head count, or for the executives to provide digital workers with the strategic guidance they need to truly take digital governance and operations in the organization to maturity.

Quantify the Risk

As I mentioned in the first chapter, sometimes organizations are so used to working the way they do that they don't understand that they are operating under substantial risk. Even 20 years into the commercial Web, digital channels are still relatively new to most organizations, and while there are emerging best practices and norms, very few digital processes can lead to a guaranteed business result. So the objective value of digital to organizations, particularly those that do not have an obvious upside from digital (like ecommerce driven and other B-to-C businesses), is sometimes difficult to express, as is the risk associated with not doing things the "right way." Despite this nebulous state, quantifying risk associated with poor digital operations and governance is not impossible, and it is a key tactic for raising concerns to senior management and executives in your organization.

When you raise risks to executives, be certain that they are substantiated with metrics. Also, make sure that the substantiation is relevant to your business. That means talking about the risk of non-compliance with accessibility standards is probably relevant to a governmental organization but less relevant to some B-to-B type organizations that do not have a legal requirement to comply with certain accessibility standards. Of course, the organization still might want to comply with those standards, but if it doesn't comply, it's not a risk (unless there is a cultural/brand risk, which could be minimized by adherence to these standards).

Another example might involve ensuring that individual customer data is handled properly online and offline. Digital has been thrown into the mix of many organizations so quickly that often they are unable to come keep track of how certain applications interact with other applications. Standards related to tracking, cookies, data management, and other privacy concerns are crucial. Yet in a decentralized digital management environment where a lot of unmanaged organic digital growth has occurred, organizations may find themselves unintentionally out of compliance. Again, this lack of compliance is not willful. It's almost accidental. However, "we didn't mean to do it" is not an effective excuse in a court of law.

Digital workers also get caught up in the correct way of doing things according to best practices. This is admirable and sometimes relevant to the business. But it's important to pick your battles. If you look around your organization, you will see that there are processes that are well done and others that are little bit looser and may not adhere to best practices. This is normal in an organization. While you always want to strive toward excellence, there are aspects of digital that are really well done and other aspects that may be not so well done. It's important for you to understand what parts you must execute upon well. From a risk perspective, those would be the policies and standards that will keep your business in alignment with the law and well positioned for profitability in your market sector.

If you are trying to challenge executives to fund additional governance initiatives or better fund digital overall, a short business argument supported by three solid but remarkable metrics is much more powerful than trying to tell the entire story of quality digital. To be honest, most executives don't want to hear tactics related to that story.

![DO'S AND DON'TS]

DON'T: Give up, just because you can't find an executive advocate for governance. There are things you can do at the grass roots level in working groups that will start to foster alignment until the executives come into alignment.

Emphasize the Business Opportunity

Many digital experts are passionate about the work they do—whether that's user-centered design, application design and development, content strategy, or mobile development. There is a right way to go about creating an effective digital presence, and digital workers understand all the details of that. But, and this might be a tough pill to swallow, often management just doesn't care about the "right way" to do something. Management wants to know how what you are proposing is going to provide quantifiable value to the organization.

I once heard Information Architecture guru Peter Morville say that executives speak in business haiku, and it's true. Executives have to be able to understand the full breadth of the business, and in order to do that, the information has to be highly distilled. Digital workers aren't always the best at distilling information. They come at their peers and managers with jargon they can't understand, spreadsheets of content, ethical diagrams, and the like. If you want executives to invest time in understanding digital, you need to take the time to understand the world of executives, which often focuses on quantifiable results. At best, you can explain how improved digital governance will help impact the bottom line, and if your executive suite isn't ready to hear that story, at the very least you can make sure that your own digital house is in order.

The first few governance projects that I worked on in the early 2000s included the U.S. Social Security Administration (SSA) and the U.S. Environmental Protection Agency (EPA), as shown in Figures 8.1 and 8.2. Both organizations had sharp Web teams. Both organizations came pretty early to the Web, and both teams were early in realizing that they had governance concerns. But the underlying dynamics of the teams were very different. At the SSA, the website had some information architecture problems, needed a new content management system, and with hindsight, probably some serious content strategy work needed to be done—the site was full of redundant, outdated, and trial (ROT) content. But the SSA's key Web manager for the public website had made a decision at the onset of digital development at the agency, which was that almost all content changes would go through his team. Technology choice decisions were also strongly centralized.

The EPA pretty much had the same set of website problems as the SSA— except more—hundreds of thousands of pages more. The site was many orders of magnitude bigger than the SSA's site. Organizationally, the EPA had (and still has) a strong "office" component (The Office of Air, The Office of Water, The Office of Solid Waste, and so on), and their digital story included office-focused distributed content, contribution rights, and technology implementation. The distribution was so complete that digital stakeholders often spoke as if those offices had completely different websites.

So the SSA had a biggish website directed mainly by a few resources, and the EPA had a huge website directed and informed by over 30 key players. Which team, do you think, had an easier time implementing governance and subsequently implementing their desired website changes? If you guessed SSA, you'd be right.

The point isn't that EPA was "wrong" and SSA was "right." The point is to illustrate that small decisions and dynamics made early in the development of a process will seriously impact a future outcome. It's the famous "Butterfly Effect" (see note: "The Butterfly Effect"). It's like drawing two sets of lines emanating from the same point, but pairing one at a 90-degree angle and the other at a 91-degree angle. If it were a short line, maybe there wouldn't be much of a difference. But if the lines were a mile long, the difference between the two lines would vary greatly from pair to pair.

In the SSA/EPA cases, the decision to centralize many governance-related decision-making functions and a lot of production to a core administrative team meant that years later the SSA had much more control over resources when it wanted to make changes. EPA was in an environment where those same choices didn't make organizational sense at conception (or simply just didn't happen), and 10 years later, they were in a completely different place regarding their ability to govern and implement website-wide change. Little things can make a big difference when you add the components of time and scale. When there are a lot of choices made that aren't documented or understood, the situation could look chaotic.

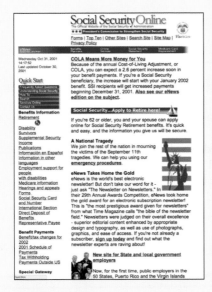

FIGURE 8.1

Social Security Administration website at the turn of the century.

FIGURE 8.2

U.S. Environmental Protection Agency website at the turn of the century.

When the present determines the future, but the approximate present does not approximately determine the future.

Edward Lorenz
(1917 – 2008)

For every organization, there have been many early decisions made about how to govern and manage digital, and those decisions have created the unique work patterns and structures that exist in your organization and online today. Every organization has a unique set of digital governance design challenges, which is why you can't skip steps. If you haven't taken the time to intentionally think about the dynamics of digital strategy, policy, standards, and digital team functions, then it will be hard to design a solid digital governance framework.

The shortcuts outlined in this chapter are helpful, but there is no substitute for the real thing. So, if you've skipped forward to this chapter, go back. It's important to do the work. It *will* make a difference. Unfortunately, you can't change the early dynamics of how digital was started in your organization, but you can understand them well *now* and begin to influence the future direction of digital. You can start the journey of navigating through your organization's unique digital chaos. You will find a way, and digital governance will improve within your organization.

Summary

- Organizations must make a conscious decision to govern well. Sometimes in order to avoid the hard work of digital, governance organizations come up with complex reasons why they cannot improve digital governing dynamics. But these dynamics are seldom the real cause for the lack of interest in digital governance. The real reasons are related to the following:

  - Not wanting to change existing work dynamics.

  - Thinking the brand is too important to fail.

  - Believing that the organization's profitability renders it bulletproof to the impact of digital.

  - Difficult people using power to make sure that the digital governance chips stay on their side of the table.

- In organizations where there is no executive support to improve digital governance, there are a few tactics that can be effective in helping improve digital operations: aligning internal digital resources at the executive, management, and digital practitioner levels of the organization; quantifying the risk of an ungoverned online presence to executives; and detailing the opportunity associated with better digital quality.

- A lot of organizations are in digital chaos, but the path they took to get to that chaos is unique. Therefore, the solution for normalizing and maturing digital governance and operations will also be unique.

PART II

Case Studies

The following are outlines of digital governance frameworks derived from projects I've worked on with clients over the past 10 years. I've combined and tweaked here and there to normalize the format of the recommendations (obviously, different organizations have different documentation needs) and to keep certain organizational and background information confidential. On the whole, though, they are realistic representations of some of the outcomes you can expect when designing your own framework.

CHAPTER 9

Multinational Business- to-Business Case Study

The "last straw" event that led this multinational business-to-business (B-to-B) organization to address digital governance was a content emergency related to inappropriate content on live websites. In trying to react to address the content concern, the executive team in the organization (20K+ employees globally) realized that there was little oversight of websites and other digital channels globally. In particular, they didn't know how many websites and social channels were being managed and moderated by the organization. There was also a general inconsistency with the quality of the content on different product and country websites. The amount of redundant, outdated, and trivial content (ROT) on the website was high, since no one had taken the opportunity to consider the full lifecycle processes for managing website content. Consequently, information was being put online and left there—for years—with no plan for maintenance or retirement of content.

This emergency led to the executive team telling the Web team to "figure it out" and come up with a content strategy and governance model. The core Web team was highly competent—one of the sharpest teams we've ever worked with. The team was already aware that there were global digital abnormalities and a lack of governance, but had never been given a clear mandate or resources to implement policy or standards for any of the other websites globally, and they lacked the bandwidth to create a framework before the crisis occurred. When we arrived, they had already performed a content audit and worked with IT to create an inventory of websites and social channels. They wanted us to help them design a governance framework with an emphasis on addressing the differing management and governance needs of various country-focused websites and their support staff.

Because of the content-centered focus of this engagement, we included a content strategist on our team to make recommendations about the organization's global content strategy as well. The company had over 20 country-specific Web and social channels that supported a number of product lines. The work of the content strategist allowed us to make deeper than usual recommendations in the arena of digital governance.

Pre-Framework Dynamics

The core digital team was frustrated that it had taken this emergency engagement to bring issues to the forefront, because they had been attempting to communicate the less positive aspects of organizational digital governance to senior management and the executive team for some time.

As we dove into our discovery process, we realized that the call for digital governance was a superficial one. In reality, the executives just wanted the website mess cleaned up. They weren't truly interested in figuring out ways to integrate digital into the business in more sophisticated ways. Here were the facts in this organization:

- Governance was perceived as solely an operational concern, not a strategic one.

- Profitability was high enough that the "upside" of digital was perceived as speculative and not an obvious channel for business opportunity.

- Funding the core team to bring more domain expertise was not likely to be a supported part of the solution. "We can't get more headcount."

- There was a high sense of geographical and brand autonomy while at the same time, given regulatory constraints around content, there was *not*, for the most part, a Wild-West type, do-your-own-thing mentality about digital content, applications, and transactions. The higher risk for the organization was out-dated, inaccurate content due to inattention and lack of strategy around content both globally and locally.

- Content needs differed from region to region, but that fact had not been taken into consideration.

These dynamics left the core digital team somewhat frustrated because they saw that there was a real opportunity for the business to become more competitive via better use of content, social software interactions, and mobile applications in the organization.

Our Overall Framework Recommendation

Given some hard constraints placed on the governance solution ("no new headcount" and some unbreakable long-term contracts with external vendors), there were limits to the solutions that we could offer. However, we were able to raise the visibility of some content concerns at various locations and recommend a more nuanced Web team model, as shown in Figure 9.1.

Multinational — Scope: *All public-facing Web and mobile sites and social media interactions*	Core						
	Executives	Information Systems	Legal	Global Compliance	Regulatory	Global Communications	Human Resources
Digital Governance Sponsorship and Advocacy							
DIGITAL STRATEGY							
Digital Strategy Definition							
DIGITAL POLICY							
Policy Stewardship				X			
Policy Authoring		X	X	X	X	X	X
DIGITAL STANDARDS							
Standards Stewardship						X	
Graphic Design—Input						X	
Graphic Design—Authors & Decision Makers						X	
Editorial Standards—Input			X		X	X	
Editorial Standards—Authors & Decision Makers					X	X	
Information Organization & Access—Input		X				X	
Information Organization & Access—Authors & Decision Makers						X	
Enterprise Tools—Input		X				X	
Enterprise Tools—Authors & Decision Makers		X				X	
Web Applications—Input		X				X	
Web Applications—Authors & Decision Makers		X					
Network & Server Infrastructure—Input		X				X	
Network & Server—Authors & Decision Makers		X					

FIGURE 9.1

Proposed B-to-B governance framework.

	Dispersed Core				Distributed			Ad Hoc	Extended						
	Country Web Manager—"Mature"	Regional Communications	Regional Regulatory	Regional Compliance	Country Web Managers—Growth	Country Web Manager—Start-up	Country Communications	Global Digital Council	Website Application Development	Mobile Application Development	Enterprise Tools	Content Maintenance	Translation Management	Website Hosting	Graphic Design
								X							
								X							
		X		X											
	X	X					X								X
		X													
	X	X	X												
		X		X											
	X	X													
	X	X										X			
	X								X	X					

Digital Team Findings and Recommendations

This organization had an array of resources working with its digital presence globally. The core team was rather sharply defined, but as we moved from the core to the outer reaches of the team, there was a lack of definition, as well as a lack of alignment with the local work at hand—particularly as it related to content development. Overall, we saw that the following circumstances were in place:

- The global digital team was ill defined, which led to poor quality in the content. Some sites had no Web manager of record and had not been updated for over 12 months. Some websites were simply "dead."

- There were loose digital development processes that were out-of-sync with industry-related compliance demands. Some content was on servers that had not been properly reviewed, or the content was outdated, which was an increasing risk to the organization.

- There were a large number of support vendors globally, but the lack of a set of codified and implemented standards did not allow for editorial consistency globally.

- Despite the increased use of digital, senior management refused to add additional headcount to the core and distributed teams in most cases.

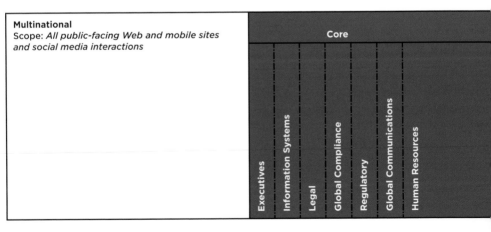

FIGURE 9.2

Digital team structure.

Our primary goal was to ensure that the digital team (see Figure 9.2) was staffed with subject matter experts who could effectively support the range of digital activities at the organization. Just as the website had grown organically, so had the team, and there was a lack of balance in the team that led directly to low user experience, especially as it related to online content.

Initially, we recommended that the organization add two additional headcount that would focus on translation management and content strategy, but this recommendation was rejected. We subsequently recommended that the organization support these activities with external vendors and via capital expenditures (instead of additional headcount).

The Core Team

The core digital team was tasked with overall guidance and direction for Web development and to ensure that the B-to-B Web presence was supported by enabling content and technical infrastructure. This team was also responsible for orchestrating all Web development processes and reporting on the effectiveness of the Web for the organization. The core digital team was placed in the Global (corporate) Communications department with technical implementation support from the Information Services teams.

Dispersed Core				Distributed			Ad Hoc	Extended							
Country Web Manager—"Mature"	Regional Communications	Regional Regulatory	Regional Compliance	Country Web Managers—Growth	Country Web Manager—Start-up	Country Communications	Global Digital Council	Website Application Development	Mobile Application Development	Enterprise Tools	Content Maintenance	Translation Management	Website Hosting	Graphic Design	

The Dispersed Core and Distributed Team

Due in large part to this B-to-B's varying business maturity and goals in various locales, different country websites had different needs online. Therefore, Web production practices and governing dynamics (like some policy and standards) needed to differ from country to country. So we needed to add a dispersed core Web team component to the framework. In particular, the dispersed core had to have accountability for some policy and standards definitions that were best defined locally.

Also, to support differing business needs, we recommended three different country Web team models within the dispersed core. One model would support countries in a "start-up" mode, another model for those in "growth" mode, and a third model for countries where B-to-B's communications, business, and sales objectives were "mature."

Start-Up

There were nine candidate countries for this category. This segment addressed digital efforts that were supporting an emerging market or a new acquisition with a light digital footprint. The core team responsibilities (governing and product-related) included the following.

Governing Responsibilities

- Global communications manager to support Web development with support from external corporate vendor of record.
- Support production-related responsibilities.
- Localize Web content when required.
- Maintain Web content within a content management system. B-to-B will provide access to resources fluent in target language who can maintain content in the CMS.
- Participate in global Web community training and networking.

Growth

There were eight candidate countries for this category. This segment addressed digital efforts for new acquisitions with a pre-existing substantive local footprint. The core team responsibilities (governing and product-related) included the following.

Governing Responsibilities

- Articulate content strategy.

- Document and clear localized Web standards with local regulatory team when they differ from corporate standards.

- Identify process for publishing and maintaining content.

- Appoint a dedicated Web manager resource *or* an active, non-dedicated communications manager.

- When in use, appoint a designated social media manager.

- Have a local Web budget to support country Web page development.

Production-Related Responsibilities

- Localize Web content when required.

- Maintain Web content within a content management system.

- Participate in global Web community training and networking.

- Update content monthly.

Mature

There were 10 candidate countries for this category, and they were candidates that had an established or strategically significant market for the company. Their core team responsibilities (governing and product-related) included the following.

Governing Responsibilities

- Localize Web budget to support country Web page development.

- Articulate content strategy.

- Define and integrate local translation management processes with the corporate Web team.

- Identify process for publishing and maintaining content.

- Document and clear localized Web standards with local regulatory team when they differ from corporate standards.

- When in use, appoint a designated social media manager.

- Appoint a dedicated Web manager resource.

Production-Related Responsibilities

- Localize Web content when required.
- Maintain Web content within B-to-B's content management system.
- Participate in global Web community training and networking.
- Update sites at least weekly.

Working Groups and Councils

There was already an established global digital council that would remain functional with the following key stakeholders:

- Regional communications managers
- Regional IT managers
- Regional business executives

Extended Team

The core team was supported by vendors who specialized in the following areas:

- Application development (website and mobile)
- Enterprise tools
- Graphic design
- Content maintenance
- Translation management (for Web)
- Website hosting

Digital Strategy/Governance Advocacy Findings and Recommendations

Digital strategy and the advocacy for deeper digital maturity were a challenge for this organization. The executives were definitely "digital conservatives," and when we left this engagement, the core team was still challenged to raise the business opportunity of digital to the executive level.

This business case for digital did not touch on the core aspects of the business model, and the somewhat sophisticated metrics that would have been required to make a business case were not at hand, nor did the core team have the bandwidth to establish those metrics. Therefore, everyone was focused on moving into the basic management phase of digital maturity, which involved understanding where their website and social channels were and who was managing them. Although they were able to better align the digital team to a set of guiding principles by the time we left, we felt that they were still not in an ideal situation. The key points of our observations were the following:

- They had a weak organizational Web strategy that was focused solely on the top-level corporate website and was driven by the Web team, not the organization at large.

- Executives were disengaged from digital unless there were "emergency" issues.

- There was a lack of alignment between the business reality and what was happening online. For example, the business had a mature and growing market with certain geographical regions, but at the same time, they were reducing the resources required to support the digital presence in that region.

Digital Strategy Accountability

We suggested that a Global Digital Council be established to serve as an advocate for deepening and maturing digital governance (see Figure 9.3). We advised that that this council should include in its charter the articulation of guiding principles and Web performance measures for Web development.

Digital Policy Findings and Recommendations

Given the highly regulated marketspace of this organization, digital policies *did* exist. However, there were weaknesses to address at the regional levels globally, which included the following:

- The digital policy stewardship was unclear.

- There was a strong corporate policy, but the digital policy concerns were not as well localized to address localized policy concerns and regulatory needs.

We recommended that policy stewardship be the responsibility of corporate compliance (see Figure 9.4). This team would assign authorship as required to regional communications staff and regional compliance officers (see Figure 9.5).

Multinational Scope: *All public-facing Web and mobile sites and social media interactions*	Core						
	Executives	Information Systems	Legal	Global Compliance	Regulatory	Global Communications	Human Resources
Digital Governance Sponsorship and Advocacy							
DIGITAL STRATEGY							
Digital Strategy Definition							

FIGURE 9.3

Accountability for digital strategy.

Multinational Scope: *All public-facing Web and mobile sites and social media interactions*	Core						
	Executives	Information Systems	Legal	Global Compliance	Regulatory	Global Communications	Human Resources
DIGITAL POLICY							
Policy Stewardship				X			
Policy Authoring		X	X	X	X	X	X

FIGURE 9.4

Accountability for digital policy.

Dispersed Core				Distributed			Ad Hoc	Extended						
Country Web Manager—"Mature"	Regional Communications	Regional Regulatory	Regional Compliance	Country Web Managers—Growth	Country Web Manager—Start-up	Country Communications	Global Digital Council	Website Application Development	Mobile Application Development	Enterprise Tools	Content Maintenance	Translation Management	Website Hosting	Graphic Design
							X							
							X							

Dispersed Core				Distributed			Ad Hoc	Extended						
Country Web Manager—"Mature"	Regional Communications	Regional Regulatory	Regional Compliance	Country Web Managers—Growth	Country Web Manager—Start-up	Country Communications	Global Digital Council	Website Application Development	Mobile Application Development	Enterprise Tools	Content Maintenance	Translation Management	Website Hosting	Graphic Design
	X		X											

Policy	Author
Accessibility	Global Communications
	Information Systems
Branding	Global Communications
Data	Information Systems
Domain Names	Information Systems
Editorial	Global Communications
	Regulatory
Email Addresses	Information Systems
Information Management	Global Communications
	Information Systems
Intellectual Property Protection	Compliance
	Legal
	Global Communications
Language & Localization	Global Communications
	Regulatory
Hyperlinks & Hyperlinking	Global Communications
	Regulatory
Privacy	Legal
	Compliance
	Regulatory
Security	Information Systems
Social Media	Global Communications
	Regulatory
	Human Resources
Web Records Management	Global Communications
	Regulatory

FIGURE 9.5
Policy authors.

Digital Standards Findings and Recommendations

This team knew that it had deficits in the area of digital standards. We wanted to help them focus on keeping standards compliance higher through clearer definition and management of the standards lifecycle. The top-level findings for this company were:

- The core digital team members were de facto stewards for corporate standards related to main business brand websites and social channels.

- The standards stewardship for distributed Web teams and websites was unclear.

- The documentation of standards was uneven with particular weaknesses with regard to information organization and access and application standards.

The corporate Web team within global communications was accountable for ensuring that all Web standards were documented and available for stakeholders to consult. The corporate Web team was also responsible for ensuring that infrastructure tools and processes were architected to support standards compliance. Finally, the corporate team was tasked to support the enforcement of Web standards by measuring and reporting compliance to standards on a quarterly basis.

Standards Input and Decision-Making

There was a high level of autonomy in this organization, so it was important to make clear how and when certain digital stakeholders would be able to provide input for certain standards. We included that level of detail in their framework summary (see Figure 9.6). Also, this team chose to be more granular about its standards areas than the four standards categories we generally outline within a framework.

After the Framework Definition

Fortunately, this team was able to informally implement its digital governance framework; however, they were not able to get the top-down executive support necessary for an across-the-board transformation that the core team desired. The upside of this situation was that all of the stakeholders were happy, for the most part, to comply with the standards as outlined by the standards "owners." Processes were tighter, and policy definition and compliance processes were much sharper, which was an essential component in this highly regulated environment. The executives were happy once the content emergency was managed.

We would have liked to have seen a more strategic engagement. But this company was doing well, and until there was an obvious disruption for the organization, it was going to be unlikely that digital would be pushed in a more strategic direction. This team is now well settled in the "basic management" stage of digital governance. And that's okay.

Multinational Scope: *All public-facing Web and mobile sites and social media interactions*	Core						
	Executives	Information Systems	Legal	Global Compliance	Regulatory	Global Communications	Human Resources
DIGITAL STANDARDS							
Standards Stewardship						X	
Graphic Design—Input						X	
Graphic Design—Authors & Decision Makers						X	
Editorial Standards—Input			X		X	X	
Editorial Standards—Authors & Decision Makers					X	X	
Information Organization & Access—Input		X				X	
Information Organization & Access—Authors & Decision Makers						X	
Enterprise Tools—Input		X				X	
Enterprise Tools—Authors & Decision Makers		X				X	
Web Applications—Input		X				X	
Web Applications—Authors & Decision Makers		X					
Network & Server Infrastructure—Input		X				X	
Network & Server—Authors & Decision Makers		X					

FIGURE 9.6

Standards accountability.

	Dispersed Core				Distributed			Ad Hoc	Extended						
	Country Web Manager—"Mature"	Regional Communications	Regional Regulatory	Regional Compliance	Country Web Managers—Growth	Country Web Manager—Start-up	Country Communications	Global Digital Council	Website Application Development	Mobile Application Development	Enterprise Tools	Content Maintenance	Translation Management	Website Hosting	Graphic Design
	X	X					X								X
		X													
	X	X	X												
		X		X											
	X	X													
	X	X										X			
	X								X	X					

Government Case Study

When we met this government organization (unidentified due to privacy issues), it was locked in a stalemate over who had authority over the look-and-feel and information architecture of its website. Certain aspects of the organization were attempting to implement a new, more integrated information architecture, and other digital stakeholders were not convinced of the proposed direction and were actively resistant. Their rationale was that the audience for the organization was too diverse to be supported by a unified information architecture and (some thought) brand identity. One team had actually created a brand new website (content and everything), but was unable to deploy it because the other team thought it was inadequate to meet the organization's needs. The Web team was caught in the middle of this debate and sought guidance to help resolve the situation. Their focus was Web only, and for this engagement, social media and mobile were intentionally excluded to avoid complexity.

To break the stalemate, we worked with the organization to create a Web governance framework for its public facing websites. The process for creating the framework included some (sometimes difficult) group conversations and workshops around policies and standards development. The team also worked internally to establish more effective communications protocols and processes across business lines.

While there was a lot of noise around the website redesign when we arrived, we were quick to notice that this was an organization with very mature processes and procedures. Also, culturally, the organization understood the values of protocols and standards. These organizational characteristics helped them to become what we felt to be one of our best success stories as it related to digital governance in a governmental organization. Many large (10K+ employees) governmental organizations have similar dynamics, but sometimes the culture or management approach is less disciplined. In those situations, implementing a governance framework can be an exceptional challenge, even when all the stakeholders agree that changes in governance need to be made. So, in this case, the very rigidity that led to their governance problems was also the source of their solution. Once the framework was defined and emplaced by leadership, the organization had a relatively easy time with implementation.

Pre-Framework Dynamics

There were very strong (and negative) opinions about digital governance in the organization. But there were two overriding themes that crystallized as we spoke with stakeholders:

- **"We don't need governance."** Many in the organization felt that a Web governance framework was not applicable because the mission of the organization's business units was too varied to support any kind of unified vision. In essence, they felt that the organization should have an array of websites that weren't necessarily related to each other in design or intent.

- **"It won't work here."** Of those people who did think that there was value in establishing mature digital governance practices, many thought that governance wouldn't work inside their organization because there were too many power brokers and independently funded silos.

These dynamics were bypassed in large part because the Web governance effort was supported by an executive level advocate who funded the digital governance project and insisted upon some of the implementation recommendations. Once the power of the framework took hold, all stakeholders could see that operating within the framework was easier and led to faster digital delivery.

Our Framework Recommendation

Overall, we recommended that this organization create a simple hub-and-spoke Web team model. The core of this team would be split between the marketing communications function and IT. The core team would maintain all key infrastructure systems like Web content management, the portal, and search engines. They would also be responsible for defining standards for the look and feel of the website. Departmental Web managers would be established and trained in order to create domain-specific departmental content. Legal teams would play a role as we formalized Web policy. The hardest aspect of this framework was the standards definition. While a simple resolution was eventually established, it took a lot of teamwork and discussion to get to the results outlined in Figure 10.1.

Due to the collaboration around the creation of the governance framework, the implementation was straightforward. The government plan was formalized at a senior level and implemented over 18 months.

Government Case Study Scope: *All public-facing websites* *(excluded mobile and social)*	Core			
	Web Team (housed in the IT department)	Information Technology (IT)—Development	Public Relations & Communications	Information Technology (IT)—Hardware and Network
STRATEGY				
Digital Governance Sponsorship and Advocacy	X			
Digital Strategy Definition				
POLICY				
Organizational Policy Stewardship				
Digital Policy Authoring	X	X	X	X
STANDARDS				
Standards Stewardship	X			
Editorial Standards—Input	X		X	
Editorial Standards—Authors & Decision Makers			X	
Graphic Design—Input	X		X	
Graphic Design—Authors & Decision Makers	X		X	
Information Organization & Access—Input	X	X	X	
Information Organization & Access—Authors & Decision Makers	X		X	
Enterprise Tools—Input	X	X	X	X
Enterprise Tools—Authors & Decision Makers	X	X		
Web Applications—Input	X	X	X	
Web Applications—Authors & Decision Makers	X	X		
Network & Server Infrastructure—Input	X	X		X
Network & Server—Authors & Decision Makers				X

FIGURE 10.1

Potential government digital governance framework.

Dispersed Core	Distributed						Committees	Extended
NO DISPERSED CORE TEAM MEMBERS	Business Unit Communication	Business Unit Vice Presidents	Business Unit Programs	Human Resources	CFO & Operations	Legal Team	NO ACCOUNTABILITY GIVEN TO COMMITTEES	NO EXTENDED WEB TEAM MEMBERS
		X						
						X		
	X		X					
	X		X					
	X		X					
	X		X					
	X		X					

Web Team Findings and Recommendations

The key Web team dynamics that we found in this government agency were somewhat typical; however, we felt that the finger-pointing at the core digital team as the root of all online quality concerns was unfair. The team had never been given any real authority to address overall website quality. In fairness, the entire organization had never holistically addressed the structure and skill set of the de facto core Web team, and we felt that it was inappropriate to attack that team for what was an organizational deficit.

The digital skill sets in the distributed team components were, on the whole, weaker than those of the resources on the core team. However, those departmental players were very influential politically and could influence the direction of the digital work stream in substantive ways. Some notable dynamics were the following:

- The primary production-focused Web team was housed within the IT department and liaised regularly with resources in communications and public relations and business unit program offices. They put up content that others in the organization created.

- Many people inside the organization questioned the competence of the core Web team. The criticism focused on basic competence: Did they really know how to make a good website? Other criticism centered on whether or not non-domain experts could curate a website with specialized content. The sentiment being

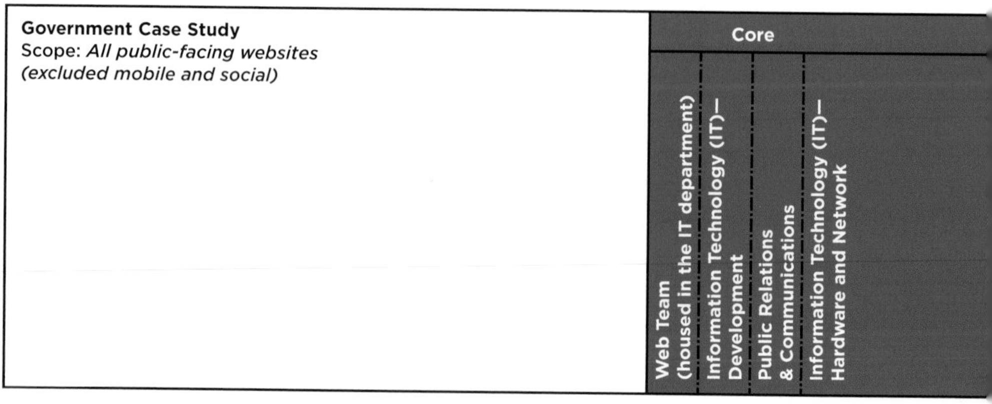

FIGURE 10.2

Recommended Web team structure.

expressed was that domain-specific knowledge experts ought to manage the website.

- The core Web team was not properly staffed. There were missing skill sets of the team members, and the team was more focused on day-to-day production rather than strategically focused on how the Web and other online channels could support the organization in meeting its goals.

- There were resources outside of the primary Web team that also had some skills in Web development. They often challenged the core Web team's authority in ways that were sometimes less than constructive, such as creating "rogue" websites that did not necessarily follow standards or best practices outlined by the core Web team.

This organization did not have a complex Web presence. There was no multilingual component aspect to the website. So areas like translation management and the workflow processes associated with it were not a factor. There were some legacy organizational units, which added some complexity, because these organizational units were not able to be dissolved, even though it seemed as if they had served their purpose and there might be a more streamlined way to manage some of the workflow processes they supported. At the end of the day, though, none of these shifts would made a difference to the digital governance or website quality. So, in order to ease implementation, we worked around this little bit of organizational complexity (see Figure 10.2).

Dispersed Core	Distributed						Committes	Extended
NO DISPERSED CORE TEAM MEMBERS	Business Unit Communication	Business Unit Vice Presidents	Business Unit Programs	Human Resources	CFO & Operations	Legal Team	NO ACCOUNTABILITY GIVEN TO COMMITTEES	NO EXTENDED WEB TEAM MEMBERS

We like to see stand-alone Web and digital teams, and this organization had one. What was unusual was that it was housed in the IT department. Usually, refined stand-alone digital teams are housed in the marketing communications departments. However, the placement of this team in IT strengthened it. IT had access to more robust funding mechanisms, and it had a more mature perspective on policy than we usually see with digital and Web teams that are housed in marketing communications teams. This is due to IT's responsibility to establish digital policy as it relates to privacy and security. Core team functions were split among the following teams with overall core team leadership from the Web team component within IT.

- Public Relations and Communications
- Web Team (housed in the IT department)
- Information Technology (IT): Development
- Information Technology (IT): Hardware and Network

Distributed Web Team

We recommended that each department Web team establish a Web manager who would be responsible for interfacing with the core Web team (see Figure 10.3). The primary responsibilities of the business unit Web managers would be content creation and maintenance. Each business unit was made responsible for funding this role. In most instances, the business units chose to fill this role with personnel from communications. Some of them hired more than one resource to fill this role, particularly if they were more active on the Web. Application development and other non-content-related production and development functions were executed from within IT components that supported the departments. Both communications and IT components followed the standards established by the core team when creating content and applications.

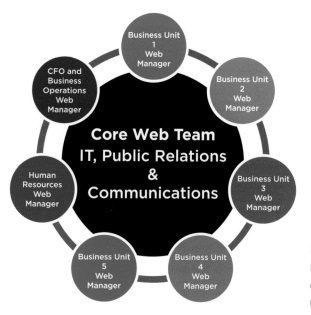

FIGURE 10.3 Recommended distributed Web team members.

Web Strategy and Governance Advocacy Findings and Recommendations

In this engagement, Web strategy really was a key. All of the stakeholders within this organization felt that they should create their own Web strategy—one that aligned with the goals and objectives of their particular business unit. But their sense of Web strategy was limited. What they really wanted to do was decide what their part of the organizational website looked like. They weren't really interested in quantifying the value the website provided to the organization or how to better operationalize aspects of the organizational agenda with the use of online tools. In some ways, this was appropriate, as there was no real obvious use case for sophisticated citizen-facing digital functionality. Still, we would have liked to see more maturity in this area. Summarized, the key findings for the Web strategy were:

- Web strategy at its highest level was not addressed. "Web strategy" inside the organization was synonymous with website structure and the look-and-feel of the site.

- There was no real sense of guiding principles or success and performance indicators.

- The executive tier was largely strategically disengaged from digital and had only been brought to the table due to a large debate regarding the look-and-feel of the public website.

- There was strong advocacy of and a call for Web governance from the very top of the organization. Leadership did not like a website stalemate and wanted the problem solved.

We recommended that accountability for Web strategy be placed at a senior management level (see Figure 10.4). Already business unit/departmental senior managers met regularly. We simply added the Web agenda to their conversation. In the future, this team will discuss how to best leverage the website in order to support the organization.

Also, this group and representatives for the core Web team will meet annually to revisit the government agency's guiding principles and ensure that they are in harmony with their organizational goals and content, data, and technology capabilities. This review was incorporated with other organization-wide objectives and metrics to ensure congruence and lack of redundancy across business unit Web efforts.

Government Case Study Scope: *All public-facing websites* *(excluded mobile and social)*	Core			
	Web Team (housed in the IT department)	Information Technology (IT)— Development	Public Relations & Communications	Information Technology (IT)— Hardware and Network
STRATEGY				
Digital Governance Sponsorship and Advocacy	X			
Digital Strategy Definition				

FIGURE 10.4

Recommendations for Web strategy accountability.

Web Policy Findings and Recommendations

We were delighted to find a legal team that was firmly engaged with digital policy. To date, the team probably had one of the most complete approaches to digital policy we have seen in our client pool. The key dynamics were:

- Web policy stewardship was not named as such, but the function was filled by the legal team. It's worth noting that this was the first organization we worked with where a member of the legal/policy team showed up for the governance framework kick-off meeting fully prepared to address policy concerns.

- Many policies had been written, particularly the IT-centered polices around privacy and security. However, many other Web-specific or content-related policy had yet to be authored. So the team needed to examine a more comprehensive list of digital policies, which they did.

We recommended that the legal team formally take on the role of policy stewards (since they were already doing such a great job). Going forward the legal team would solicit input from policy authors for subject-matter-specific content (for example, information

Dispersed Core	Distributed						Committes	Extended
NO DISPERSED CORE TEAM MEMBERS	Business Unit Communication	Business Unit Vice Presidents	Business Unit Programs	Human Resources	CFO & Operations	Legal Team	NO ACCOUNTABILITY GIVEN TO COMMITTEES	NO EXTENDED WEB TEAM MEMBERS
		X						

Government Case Study Scope: *All public-facing websites* *(excluded mobile and social)*	Core			
	Web Team (housed in the IT department)	Information Technology (IT)— Development	Public Relations & Communications	Information Technology (IT)— Hardware and Network
POLICY				
Organizational Policy Stewardship				
Digital Policy Authoring	X	X	X	X

FIGURE 10.5

Recommended policy accountability.

related to branding or technological capabilities). After policies were drafted, they would be codified through the normal organizational policy codification process at the organization and referenced on the employee intranet (see Figure 10.5).

Standards authors: (policy authoring would be broken out among the following teams):

- Public Relations and Communications
- Web Team (housed in the IT department)
- Information Technology (IT): Development
- Information Technology (IT): Hardware and Network

Web Standards Findings and Recommendations

Digital stakeholders were engaged in the typical debate around who gets to determine website standards. As with the strategy component, all stakeholders felt that they should be able to establish their standards locally in their own department. After the initial framework engagement, we did a more substantial drill down on

Dispersed Core	Distributed						Committes	Extended
NO DISPERSED CORE TEAM MEMBERS	Business Unit Communication	Business Unit Vice Presidents	Business Unit Programs	Human Resources	CFO & Operations	Legal Team	NO ACCOUNTABILITY GIVEN TO COMMITTEES	NO EXTENDED WEB TEAM MEMBERS
						X		

roles and responsibilities around website standards. Those roles have been adopted, and the debates have ceased. Some particular Web standards dynamics were:

- There was no steward for digital standards identified.

- The organization had strong standards for design and editorial.

- Standards related to information organization and access, Web tools and applications, and network and server infrastructure standards were weaker.

- Most of the standards' lifecycles (define, disseminate, implement, and measure) were largely unaddressed.

- Due to a lack of maturity in standards, there was a lot of debate around things like the look-and-feel of the site and what sorts of infrastructure tools, like Web content management systems and search engines, ought to be procured and implemented.

Once most of the concerns regarding standards ownership were aired, we introduced the concept of input versus decision-making. The team adopted the following responsibilities with ease:

Standards Steward: Web Team (housed in the IT department).
See Figure 10.6.

Government Case Study Scope: *All public-facing websites* *(excluded mobile and social)*	Core			
	Web Team (housed in the IT department)	Information Technology (IT)—Development	Public Relations & Communications	Information Technology (IT)—Hardware and Network
STANDARDS				
Standards Stewardship	X			
Editorial Standards—Input	X		X	
Editorial Standards—Authors & Decision Makers			X	
Graphic Design—Input	X		X	
Graphic Design—Authors & Decision Makers	X		X	
Information Organization & Access—Input	X	X	X	
Information Organization & Access—Authors & Decision Makers	X		X	
Enterprise Tools—Input	X	X	X	X
Enterprise Tools—Authors & Decision Makers	X	X		
Web Applications—Input	X	X	X	
Web Applications—Authors & Decision Makers	X	X		
Network & Server Infrastructure—Input	X	X		X
Network & Server—Authors & Decision Makers				X

FIGURE 10.6

Web standards roles.

Dispersed Core	Distributed						Committes	Extended
NO DISPERSED CORE TEAM MEMBERS	Business Unit Communication	Business Unit Vice Presidents	Business Unit Programs	Human Resources	CFO & Operations	Legal Team	NO ACCOUNTABILITY GIVEN TO COMMITTEES	NO EXTENDED WEB TEAM MEMBERS
	X		X					
	X		X					
	X		X					
	X		X					
	X		X					

Standards Authors:

- Public Relations and Communications

- Web Team (housed in the IT department)

- Information Technology (IT): Development

- Information Technology (IT): Hardware and Network

Key "Input" Stakeholders:

- Business Unit Communication

- Business Unit Programs

Two Years Later

Two years after implementing this framework, the organization has been able to normalize the majority of the public website's look-and-feel, and the team communicates well. The Web team has adopted an incremental approach to standards definition and implementation. A number of key standards have been documented and are supported by all internal stakeholders. The framework implementation has been effective because the organization, as a whole, now sees the value of a standards-based approach to development and perceives Web governance as an enabler, not a roadblock. The team has also come to see the value of a unified approach to Web standards.

Higher Education Case Study

From a business perspective, this 9,000-student research university was suffering from many of the symptoms that come along with the digital disruption in higher education. They were struggling to understand how deeply and when to adopt online coursework; how to effectively engage a student body of digital natives *and* the body of institutional donors that supported the university financially; and how much of the internal processes related to admissions, registration, and physical operations should be converted to a more progressive digital framework. No easy answers here.

More tactically, the university found it difficult to coordinate the digital efforts of the entire campus. As in any university setting, there were a number of strong players, including admissions, communications, and the IT department (in which the core digital team was housed) that were particularly invested in the direction of digital. There were multiple "official" websites that served different and sometimes overlapping functions. And, as is often the case in a higher education environment, there were a number of other players on the periphery that added to the digital governance dynamics. Some professors at the university had developed their own websites and social media channels to promote their personal academic achievements, and some departments had university students piloting digital functionality that worked well for a department but was not integrated with the rest of the university's digital channels.

An executive-level resource brought our team in to try and iron out some of these digital governance and operational concerns and bring the university-wide team into alignment.

Pre-Framework Dynamics

At its core, the university was suffering from a serious user experience concern: how do we manage the full user experience with the university including digital? Digital development was seen as a disintegrated series of tactical concerns. And, as with most universities, there were a number of legacy processes, like admissions and registration, which were ironed deeply into staffing models and budgetary allocation schemes. Interesting dynamics included the following:

- Although all were aware of how digital had disrupted the higher education market, they were hard pressed to align strategically to make the pivot required.

- Their IT team was sure that it was appropriate for them to write Web content without the participation of communications.

- There was an intellectual understanding of the value of a unified approach of digital to governance, but a tactical reluctance to change existing processes and align collaboratively across organizational silos.

- Due to a lack of strategy, practically any university stakeholder could insist that functionality be implemented.

Our Overall Framework Recommendation

The leadership at this organization expressed a strong desire to do things comprehensively with the role of digital in the university. So we dug deep and recommended that this institution consider the full range of experiences that students and alumni might have with the university and how digital might enhance them. We took an aggressive approach toward disseminating digital throughout the broader organization in all aspects of governance (see Figure 11.1).

Organization: Higher Education / Description of Scope: *All Digital Channels*	Core				Distributed			Committees	
	Office of the Provost/User Experience	Communications	Office of the CIO/IT	University Executives	Departments	Library	Faculty	Digital University Consortium	Digital University CoP
STRATEGY									
Digital Govenance Sponsorship and Advocacy				X					
Digital Strategy Definition	X							X	
Digital Strategy—Guiding Principles				X					
Digital Strategy—Metrics	X								
POLICY									
Organizational Poicy Stewardship			X						
Digital Policy Authoring	X	X	X						
STANDARDS									
Standards Stewardship	X								
Digital Standards Input					X	X	X		X
Digital Standards Definition—Design	X	X							
Digital Standards Definition—Editorial	X	X							
Digital Standards Definition—Publishing & Development	X		X						
Digital Standards Definition—Network & Infrastructure			X						

FIGURE 11.1

Proposed higher education framework.

Digital Team Findings and Recommendations

The digital team within IT was staffed was experienced platform developers, most of whom had long-term Web development experience. This team was expected to execute within the full range of functions required for maintaining the university's websites. That meant that application and platform developers were making decisions about content, information architecture, and what projects were implemented. This behavior harked back to the old-school traditional "webmaster" role that was prevalent in the earlier days of website development when a single resource was expected to manage an organization's Web presence. This model was no longer effective at the university and needed to be adjusted so that those with domain expertise in content, user experience, and technology would be better able to contribute their specialized skills to the development and maintenance of the university's digital campus. Some other concerns were the following:

- A disconnect existed between the articulated importance of digital and the staffing of the Web team.

- Digital team skills and expertise were incomplete.

- There was a strong digital *project* focus, but the sense of digital *operations* that existed to support ongoing infrastructure activities was absent.

- The project prioritization process did not exist, so many projects languished in the pipeline for years.

The Core Team

This university's core Web team was housed in IT. In general, the team was a bit tone-deaf to the overall needs of the organization—despite a genuine desire to do good work. In many organizations, the Web or digital team complained about different organizational "silos" that wanted to do their own thing as it related to digital. In this case, it was the Web team that was operating in a silo. There were a lot of good practices that were in play, but much of the digital development activity seemed out of sync with the organizational needs (as perceived by other digital stakeholders).

In order to distribute the digital development effort more effectively throughout the university, we recommended that the university spread the core team function in the following manner (see Figure 11.2):

- Create a digital strategy/user experience function within the Provost's office.
- Establish a content strategy function in communications.
- Focus IT resources on defining and maintaining the digital platform.

Organization: Higher Education Description of Scope: *All Digital Channels*	Core				Distributed			Commit-tees	
	Office of the Provost/User Experience	Communications	Office of the CIO/IT	University Executives	Departments	Library	Faculty	Digital University Consortium	Digital University CoP
STRATEGY									
Digital Govenance Sponsorship and Advocacy				X					
Digital Strategy Definition	X							X	
Digital Strategy—Guiding Principles				X					
Digital Strategy—Metrics	X								

FIGURE 11.2
Digital team defined.

User Experience Function

We recommended the establishment of a user experience function within the Office of the Provost. The aim of this function was to coordinate and integrate disparate university processes so that the university could deliver a quality and effective experience to its community wherever they were and whatever they were doing—whether that was an online interaction or a real-world interaction or a combination of both.

Key to this function would be to establish mechanisms for collaboration around systems and processes at the university. This function would go beyond simply improving the quality of the Web at the university. It would point toward a long-term vision of more efficient, cost-effective operations that leveraged the capabilities of digital platforms to meet the changing expectations of faculty, staff, students, and alumni.

Here were the roles of focus and development.

Manager of Digital Strategy and User Experience

- Provides overall digital standards stewardship.

- Defines development and publishing standards.

- Understands the constellation of university social media accounts, Web and mobile sites, and their interactions.

- Ensures consistent and good user experience across all digital platforms and real-world endeavors.

- Defines specific digital performance metrics to align with top tasks and other performance measures.

- Embraces stewardship of the university website domains and social accounts registry.

- Identifies and manages the vendor of record to execute on digital projects as needed.

- Chairs the digital consortium.

- Drafts the digital plan.

Metrics Analyst

- Maintains standards wiki.

- Executes user experience and analytics measurement tactics.

- Liaises with IT to define and implement Web analytics tool platform.

User Experience Coordinator

- Ensures timely and successful implementation of digital projects.

- Identifies project effectiveness analytics and project use case.

- Coordinates IT, communications, and external vendors for implementation of new Web functional or major functionality revisions.

- Supports the content strategy manager with the managing of the digital university community of practice.

Content Strategy Function (Communications)

We considered communications to be the natural home of content strategy with its focus on editorial content and ability to deliver the right information and content to the right audience.

Roles of focus and development were the following.

Content Strategy (Manager)

- Defines digital content strategy for all digital channels.

- Acts as a consultant for projects (rich media development and content).

- Defines digital editorial standards.

- Oversees digital content strategy.

- Manages information architecture.

- Serves as a member of the digital university consortium.

Editorial Support

- Maintains content and supports editorial.

- Moderates and supports social media.

Digital Graphic Design

- Vendor of record.

Focus IT Resources on Platform

IT's natural domain is systems support and development. We recommended that the Web team within IT continue to maintain and grow the Web technology platform, including Web content management, portal, and search and analytics software.

Roles of focus and development were the following.

Digital Platform Management and Development

- Implements and sustains tools required for the digital platform, supporting Web, mobile, and social interactions.

- Ensures that the university has an appropriate and usable platform that meets the content authoring and delivery needs of the university community as defined by the digital plan.

- Defines publishing and development and network and server Web standards.

- Manages enterprise Web tool vendors as needed.

- Liaises with external IT resources/vendors to ensure standards compliance.

- Coordinates tool-related training and implementation tactics.

Manager

- Oversees the platform program and product management.

- Serves as a digital consortium member.

- Delivers digital publishing, development, and delivery architecture for the university.

- Develops and defines tool standards.

- Defines network and server infrastructure standards.

- Inputs and makes decisions for network and server infrastructure standards.

The Distributed Team

The university needed to ensure that its faculty and staff were enabled to maintain their own Web content and moderate their own social channels as required. As it stood, content contributors were frustrated by the Web content management platform interface and often chose not to maintain their content. The result was that the Web team spent a lot of time making edits to content when others could have executed that task more easily. So it was important that content contributors extended their existing skill set in order to learn how to use the existing Web content management systems and other tools that might be implemented in the future.

We recommended that the university do the following:

- Require faculty and staff to maintain and support their own Web content and moderate their own social media accounts.

- Establish ownership of content maintenance with individual contributors and subject matter experts.

Working Groups and Committees

We recommended two new collaborative entities at the university: the Digital University Consortium and the Digital University Community of Practice (COP). The Consortium was strategically focused. The COP was practitioner focused. As it stood, the two communities of stakeholders were blended, and we felt that caused unnecessary discussion and debate over production concerns and not enough concentrated focus on the overall university digital strategy.

Digital University Consortium

We suggested the establishment of a Web community of practice whose main function was to keep collaboration active among the large number of specialists that supported the Web at the university—including students, faculty, and dedicated digital team members.

The Digital University Consortium was tasked to explore opportunities to transform or enhance legacy organizational processes via emerging digital technologies. Recommended membership included:

- University user experience manager (chair)
- Representative from research
- Representative from the registrar's office
- Representative from the library
- Content strategy manager
- Digital platform lead
- IT systems
- Human resources
- Facilities
- Housing
- Faculty membership (rotating)

Advisors/Sounding Boards

- CIO
- Director of Communications

Immediate Agenda

- Sketch guiding principles to jump-start and focus conversations about digital.

- Rationalize approach to digital budget. (Define what is a shared cost versus what is a "department-specific fee for service.")

- Integrate and synthesize organization-wide "big" digital requirements.

- Provide input for university digital, technical architecture, and content strategy plans.

- Discuss pros and cons of adopting a university-wide, services-oriented application architecture and agile development environment.

- Examine and discuss the TBD list of digital projects to be implemented by the Web team. Remove unnecessary items and find opportunities for consolidation.

Digital University CoP

We recommended that the university institute a community of practitioners that had an interest in the university's digital campus. This community could include content contributors, students, and faculty. The content strategy manager would lead this community. Meetings should be held no less than quarterly.

Unlike the University Digital Consortium, whose purpose was to collaborate in order to make strategic recommendations to leadership (and with a limited membership), the Community of Practice would serve as an open forum in which to showcase aspects of the digital campus under development. The purpose of this community would be to share information about university Web initiatives and emerging best practices. It would also provide a forum for training related to standards and industry best practices in Web management, and it would serve as a venue for innovators to showcase new digital work being done at the university.

Digital Strategy Findings and Recommendations

During the discovery process, all stakeholders articulated the importance of better and more productive management of the digital campus. But during our discovery, we determined that many pre-Web management practices still existed and were being sustained even in areas where leadership and the Web development team realized there was an opportunity to either improve the online face of the university or otherwise create advantages. Also, there was some incongruence between an articulated desire to improve the digital presence and the size of the existing Web team—the Web team had shrunk, not grown, over recent years, despite the backlog of projects, some of which had been on the list for well over a year.

The university did not really have a digital plan to articulate how it would leverage digital channels to support core operations, communications, and transactions. This oversight was also reflected in some general confusion among some digital stakeholders about how digital development efforts were funded or what a funding model should be.

The end result was a "governance by power" scenario where those with budget and authority often got their way online—for good and for bad. Some of the specific dynamics were:

- No documented digital strategy existed.

- The digital funding model was unclear or not understood by key stakeholders.

- Metrics to measure effectiveness and quality were absent.

- Decision-making for digital standards and digital portfolio was unclear.

Accountability/Responsibility for Digital Strategy

We recommended that accountability (see Table 11.1) for ensuring that a digital strategy was implemented at the university and resided with the university executive leadership (see Figure 11.3).

Tactics for executing on digital strategy included:

- Establish a Digital University Consortium as a forum for strategic collaboration.

- Create a digital governance framework to clarify university digital roles and responsibilities.

- Draft and approve a digital plan.

- Establish digital guiding principles.

- Clarify the digital budget.

- Define metrics for measuring digital effectiveness.

TABLE 11.1 DIGITAL STRATEGY ACCOUNTABILITY

Actor	Accountability
Executive Leadership	Codify and socialize digital guiding principles.
	Codify and emplace digital governance framework.
	Define guiding principles to align with the university culture, the institutional plan, and the faculty and departmental needs.
	Implement and maintain a digital budget strategy.
	Define digital governance framework and recommend it to the president for codification.
	Approve the digital plan.
	Monitor the success of the digital plan.
Office of the Provost	Draft the digital plan.
	Establish a metrics framework and measure digital quality and effectiveness.
University Digital Consortium	Provide input to and frame the digital plan.
	Brainstorm digital scenarios and use cases to inform the digital budget strategy.

Organization: Higher Education Description of Scope: *All Digital Channels*	Core				Distributed			Committees	
	Office of the Provost/User Experience	Communications	Office of the CIO/IT	University Executives	Departments	Library	Faculty	Digital University Consortium	Digital University CoP
STRATEGY									
Digital Govenance Sponsorship and Advocacy				X					
Digital Strategy Definition	X							X	
Digital Strategy—Guiding Principles				X					
Digital Strategy—Metrics	X								

FIGURE 11.3

Accountability for digital structure.

Digital Policy Findings and Recommendations

The university seemed to understand the impact of digital and the need to manage the associated risk. However, the "last mile" needed to be covered by formal documentation to ensure that the substance of their policy was socialized throughout the organization.

- A digital policy steward needed to be identified to "own" the creation and maintenance of policies.

- The university had much of the information required to create a best practices set of digital policy, but it had not formally documented these policies.

- Some pre-existing policies, such as records management, needed to be re-examined to ensure that they were still effective in the wake of the growth of digital.

The university had a handle on identifying areas where digital policy was required, and for the most part, information existed to support the drafting of a formal policy. Also, the role of digital policy stewardship was clearly defined within the Office of Finance and Administration. The CIO's office had a keen eye toward emerging trends on the Internet and World Wide Web, as well as region-specific university systems.

Our suggestions included the following:

- Place stewardship for digital policy with the CIO's office.

- Formalize digital policies and aggregate them with other university policies.

- Develop formal Web policies in a standard format and cross-reference them with existing university policies and supporting standards where feasible.

- Review existing policies for impact by the establishment of new digital channels.

The university *had* much of the information required to draft policy. Therefore, we recommended that it actively do so and publish that information in an area that was easily findable and accessible to university digital stakeholders—as some of the existing policy information was difficult to discover. Also, we recommended that plain-language summaries of the policy be provided for those who were simply trying to understand the thrust of the policy, such as external support vendors and casual content contributors within the university.

We felt that primary stewardship for the digital policy definition rested with the Office of the CIO, as that function was uniquely qualified to understand both the internal and external drivers that might impact the substance of the university digital policy. However, authorship of policy should be delegated to Communications, IT, User Experience, and Records Management resources as required (see Figure 11.4).

Organization: Higher Education Description of Scope: *All Digital Channels*	Core				Distributed			Committees	
	Office of the Provost/User Experience	Communications	Office of the CIO/IT	University Executives	Departments	Library	Faculty	Digital University Consortium	Digital University CoP
POLICY									
Organizational Poicy Stewardship			X						
Digital Policy Authoring	X	X	X						

FIGURE 11.4
Accountability for digital policy.

Digital Standards Findings and Recommendations

Like many organizations, the university had done an uneven job of documenting its standards. The lack of documented standards caused a lot of confusion and contention within the university community:

- Decision-making authority for standards was assumed and unclear.

- Design and editorial standards were lightly documented.

- Publishing and development and network and server infrastructure standards were poorly documented.

The university had begun to document digital design and editorial standards, but standards related to the digital publishing platform, portals, search engines, and other more technically focused concerns remained undefined and undocumented. Over the years, the core Web team (within IT) had assumed authority for defining many standards. But because this authority was assumed and not formally granted, often there was "pushback" from university stakeholders who had differing views.

Organization: Higher Education Description of Scope: *All Digital Channels*	Core				Distributed			Committees	
	Office of the Provost/User Experience	Communications	Office of the CIO/IT	University Executives	Departments	Library	Faculty	Digital University Consortium	Digital University CoP
STANDARDS									
Standards Stewardship	X								
Digital Standards Input					X	X	X		X
Digital Standards Definition—Design	X	X							
Digital Standards Definition—Editorial	X	X							
Digital Standards Definition—Publishing & Development	X		X						
Digital Standards Definition—Network & Infrastructure			X						

FIGURE 11.5

Digital standards.

We recommended that overall stewardship of standards sit with the User Experience function within the Provost's office (see Figure 11.5). We also recommended the input and decision-making authoring responsibilities be divided as follows:

- **Design:** Communications and the Office of the Provost (see Table 11.2)

- **Editorial:** Communications and the Office of the Provost (see Table 11.3)

- **Publishing and Development:** Office of the CIO and Office of the Provost (see Table 11.4)

- **Network and Server Infrastructure:** Office of the CIO (see Table 11.5)

TABLE 11.2 GRAPHIC DESIGN DECISION-MAKING

Stakeholder	Input	Decision
Communications	X	X
Office of the Provost (User Experience)	X	X

TABLE 11.3 EDITORIAL DECISION-MAKING

Stakeholder	Input	Decision
Communications	X	X
Office of the Provost (User Experience)	X	X
Faculties/Admin	X	

TABLE 11.4 PUBLISHING AND DEVELOPMENT DECISION-MAKING

Stakeholder	Input	Decision
Communications Content Strategy	X	
Office of the CIO Digital Platform	X	X
Office of the Provost User Experience	X	X
Registrar's Office	X	
Library	X	
Content Contributor Representatives	X	

TABLE 11.5 NETWORK AND SERVER DECISION-MAKING

Stakeholder	Input	Decision
Communications	X	
Office of the CIO – Infrastructure Systems & Digital Platform		X
Office of the Provost User Experience	X	
Registrar's Office	X	
Library	X	
Administration	X	

What Happened After We Left

The university agreed with our recommendations, but had difficulty finding internal sponsorship to implement all the staffing changes recommended effectively. This was interesting because the project was sponsored at a fairly senior level of the organization. However, this team is still firmly committed to its governance journey. There is strong collaboration and alignment among the core team members, and they have taken steps to define and implement digital standards effectively. They are also in the process of developing a formal university-wide community of practice that will recommend guiding principles to leadership. While not exactly our recommendation, they are moving in a positive direction.

We felt that the external business drivers and competition to this organization were not strong enough to engage executives (despite their sponsorship of this project). It is good, though, that the digital team is aligning around governance good practices. When digital hits the higher education sector more directly, this organization will be prepared to act.

CODA
YOU—THIS TIME NEXT YEAR

Imagine this. You're a director of digital for a multinational organization or a university or a government organization. (Anywhere. It's your fantasy). You come to work one day and dial in to your monthly digital community of practice meeting where you and representatives from the global digital team discuss content strategy, the new shared CMS you are selecting and implementing. You hear a story from one of the country website managers about a new ecommerce initiative and openly discuss how others in the organization may join in the effort or leverage their knowledge. You report on how some new business initiatives from corporate might impact some of the digital standards your team has established—and then the team has a discussion about it. No one is arguing with you about your authority to make a decision. No one is threatening to build a rogue website on the side. You're collaborating. You're acting as a team. You're governing well, with intent.

This story is real. This head of digital went from "I have no idea what's going on" and complete chaos to effective governance in less than a year.

And you can do it, too.

INDEX

training people in organization, 36
user experience coordinator, 203–204
user experience function, 202–204
corporate governance
aligning with fiscal management, 115
doing well, 114
dynamics, 113–115
influencing digital governance, 114
multiple styles of, 114–115
not doing well, 113–114
"tail wagging the dog," 114
corporate policy and digital policy, 13
corporate websites, 4
councils, 43, 46
authority, 32
budgeting, 32
governance-focused, 46
multinational business-to-business
(B2B) case study, 172
responsibilities, 43
roles, 32
creativity standards, 94

D

decision-making
authority for final decision
constituency, 107
digital standards, 177
exercise, 108–109
versus input, 106–108
interest constituency, 107
decision-making authority, 9–11
design, 22
design team
leadership, 133
membership, 134–135
populating for digital governance
framework, 132–135
working group, 135
development
framework for coherent, 92
protocols, 22
difficult people, 148–149
digital
administrative side of, 34–36
cutting-edge work, 61

development and digital policy, 73
inability of digital teams to
present case for digital to
executives, 54–55
integrating regular business
processes into, 61
organizational culture toward, 12
organizational response to, 54–56
organizations disrupted by, 60–61
organizations missing target in, 147
organization's statement of
approach to, 57
outsourcing, 58
product or service as, 58
quantifying risk, 153–155
siloed approach to development, 35
steering general direction of, 151–152
strategic aspects for organization,
57–58
digital analytics, 62
digital center of excellence, 152
digital community of practice (CoP),
100, 152–153
digital conservatives, 63–64, 66
digital development DNA, 10
digital disruption, 148–149
digital experts
cutting-edge work, 61
informing digital strategy, 59
strategic aspects of digital for
organization, 57–58
digital governance
brands, products, and programs local
concerns, 39–40
buying IT systems to solve
problems, 49
definition of, 11
difficult people, 148–149
digital center of excellence, 152
digital community of practice
(CoP), 152–153
digital maturity curve, 24–25
digital steering committee, 151–152
distinction from digital
production, 141
emphasizing business
opportunity, 155

digital worker role, 56–57
expressing standards, 92
guiding principles, 11, 54
handing off to digital team, 57
higher education case
    study, 208–209
leadership role, 56
leading and owning by
    organization, 58
multinational business-to-business
    (B2B) case study, 172–173
need for separate, 58–61
off target, 12
organizational culture toward
    digital, 12
organization's inability to define and
    execute, 55
performance measures
    development, 57
performance objectives, 11, 54
qualitative factors, 55
quantitative factors, 55
responsibilities, 208–209
set of resources, 12
statement of organization's approach
    to digital, 57
team, 12
who should define, 56–58
digital teams, 24, 31
authority, 32
basic management skills lack, 55
budgeting for, 32
clearly defined roles, 32
committees, 43, 46
core teams, 33–40
councils, 32, 43, 46
definition of, 32
digital knowledge, 105–106
digital steering committees, 32
distributed digital team, 41–43
expanded members of, 32
extended digital team, 32, 46–47
external vendor support, 47
handing off digital strategy to, 57
higher education case study, 201
inability present strategic case for
    digital to executives, 54–55

incorrectly defined by
    organizations, 32
individuals making up, 31–32
intermingling people with
    institutional knowledge and
    business savvy with digital
    expertise, 55–56
location, 32
make-up of, 35
people resources, 56
professional development lack, 35
properly resourced, 34
reviewing digital policy, 83
role, 32
understanding digital, 55
well-organized *versus* poorly
    organized, 33
working groups, 32, 43, 46
Digital University Community of
    Practice (CoP), 206, 207
Digital University Consortium,
    206–207
digital workers
    digital strategy role, 56–57
    disruption, 62
    forward point of view, 150
    less than ideal
        circumstances, 150–151
    measuring digital standards
        compliance, 102
    versus policy steward, 76
    right way to do something, 155
    stifling expertise, 150
director or vice president of digital, 35
dispersed core team in multinational
    business-to-business (B2B) case
    study, 170
disruptive innovation concept, 52–53
distributed digital team, 41–43
    higher education case study, 205
    multinational business-to-business
        (B2B) case study, 170
distributed Web team and government
    case study, 188
domain names, 17
    digital policy, 79
    registration and management, 119

non-profit organizations
   consensus decision-making, 144
   we're too important to fail, 146
Nordstrom, 59–60
Norton, Edward, 91
Number Resource Organization (NRO), 119

O

office of the president, 131
Office of the Provost, 202
organizational culture
   casual, 121
   collaboration, 120–121
   digital governance framework, 120, 122
   for-profit environment, 121
   government case study, 182
   hierarchical, top-down decision-making, 121
   shifts due to impact of digital, 121
   what is possible in organization, 121
organizations
   ability to transform, 112
   behaviors and development activities, 74
   compulsory separations, 116
   difficult people, 148–149
   digital center of excellence, 152
   digital community of practice (CoP), 152–153
   digital disruptions, 149
   digitally conservative leadership, 147
   digital policy protecting, 13, 73, 78
   digital steering committee, 151–152
   digital strategy, 55, 58
   digital system working on many different levels, 36–37
   disconnected from trends in Internet and World Wide Web (WWW), 118–119
   disrupted by digital, 60–61, 121
   emphasizing business opportunity, 155
   existing dynamics *versus* digital demands, 112

geography-related demands, 116–118
global, 116–117
healthy cash reserve, 147
immature digital governance, 42
incorrectly defining digital teams, 32
integrating regular processes into digital, 61
legacy business metrics to measuring performance, 62
market-specific demands, 115–116
missing target in digital, 147
moving forward in less than ideal circumstances, 150–151
nature of digital presence, 123, 125
negative management, 148–149
not staffing bridging function well, 47
owner bloating requirements, 47
quantifying risk, 153–155
response to digital matters, 54–56
risk-taking, 80
serving core interests, 13
standards compliance, 95
statement of approach to digital, 57
strategic aspects of digital for, 57–58
successful and managerial hubris, 53
transformation is too hard, 145
underestimating transformation, 147
understanding applications, websites, and social channels used by, 123
unsophisticated digital presence and core team, 42
vital business systems not disrupted by digital, 61
we're too important to fail, 146
we're too profitable to fail, 148
outsourcing digital, 58

P

Pausch, Randy, 91
Pelz-Sharpe, Alan, 49
performance measures, 57, 62
performance objectives, 11
personal privacy, 119
planned communities, 90–91
Podnar, Kristina, 86

policy authors
  assigning responsibilities, 77–80
  communications department, 78
  consulting with right resources, 78
  distributed across organization, 78
  IT department, 78
  legal department, 78
  marketing department, 78
policy stewards, 120, 210–211
  characteristics, 76
  digital policy, 83
  digital risk, 77
  identifying, 75–77
  Internet and World Wide Web
    (WWW) governance, 118–119
  legal department, 76–77
  responsibilities, 76
  Web policy, 191–192
privacy, 17
  digital policy, 79
  personal, 119
  websites, 70–71
privacy policies, 71
procedures, 97
producers, 46
product as digital, 58
product management core team, 36–37
program management
  addressing full scope of digital, 35
  administrative side of digital, 34–36
  core team, 34–36
  hyper-focus on production, 35
  minimizing or dismissing, 35
  resources, 34–35
  weak, 34
project managers, 46
public affairs, 131
publishing and development, 22
publishing and media industry lack
  of reaction to World Wide Web
    (WWW), 53
publishing digital content, 141

Q

quantifying risk, 153–155

R

Ready, Internet, Go!, 4
records retention policies, 72
Redbox, 53, 147
redundant, outdated, and trial (ROT)
  content, 156–157, 164
registrar, 131
requirements, keeping business owner
  from bloating, 47
research-focused organizations, 144
resources
  bridging with facilitators with no
    governing authority, 46, 47
  debate about substance and content of
    digital standards, 104
  focusing IT resources on
    platform, 204–205
  micromanaging and
    overburdening, 47
responsibilities
  committees, 43
  core team, 38–40
  councils, 43
  digital authorship, 77–80
  digital strategy, 208–209
  policy steward, 76
  standards authors, 104
  standards steward, 95
  well-defined, 34
  working groups, 43
Reynolds, Malvina, 90
risk, quantifying, 153–155
risk management, 13
Rockley, Ann, 109
roles, 11
  core team, 37
  councils, 32
  digital steering committees, 32
  digital teams, 32
  well-defined, 34
  working groups, 32
Ross, Jeanne, 107
Rouse, James, 91

S

scope creep, 47
scrum managers, 46
security, 17, 70–71
  digital policy, 79
  network and server, 23
senior IT manager, 35
senior marketing manager, 35
server hardware, 23
server software, 23
service as digital, 58
Sinton, Chris, 4
social digital metrics, 62
social media, 17
  digital policy, 79
social media policies, 71
Social Security Administration (SSA),
  156–157
sponsor for digital governance
  framework, 128–131
standardization, 90–92
standards
  See also digital standards
  authority for defining, 93
  collaboration, 94
  compliance, 95
  compliance measurement, 101–102
  core team, 95–96
  creativity, 94
  determining what should be, 99
  documenting, 103
  ecommerce, 93
  enabling rapid growth, 92
  framing and limiting what you can do,
    92–93
  growth and, 94
  leveraging already documented, 99
  taking stress out of development, 93
  who has authority to define, 93
standards authors
  characteristics, 102
  identifying, 102–106
  responsibilities, 104
  Web standards, 193
standards framework, 92

standards operating procedures, 97
standards steward, 120
  characteristics, 95
  identifying, 95–96
  implementing standards, 100–101
  Internet and World Wide Web (WWW)
    governance, 118–119
  responsibilities, 95
  understanding existing standards, 99
  Web standards, 193
steering committees,
  governance-focused, 46
structured reusable content, 109

T

technical team digital policy, 72
templates, 22
terms-of-use, 70–71
"The Last Lecture: Really Achieving
  Your Childhood Dreams," 91
tools, 22
traditional print publishing shifting
  to all or near-all digital product
  delivery, 58
transformation, underestimating, 147
transformation is too hard, 145
Tyler, Jan Johnston, 4
typography and color, 22

U

unintentional digital
  conservatives, 63–64
unintentional digital progressives, 65
The United Nations (UN), 119
universities
  intellectual autonomy and
    stubbornness of staff, 144
  we're too important to fail, 146
user experience, 54
user experience coordinator, 203–204
user experience experts, 46, 55
user experience function, 202–204

ACKNOWLEDGMENTS

There were three categories of people who supported me while I wrote *Managing Chaos*: those people who encouraged me to get started; those who helped me make the book better; and those who poked and prodded me to the finish line. Only one person fits all three of those categories: Lou Rosenfeld. Thanks, Lou. You help people do good work and actualize their potential, and that's rare and important work.

For those who helped me get started, I'll name my son Rhys Welchman who has been present and supportive in every incarnation of my work in digital and always believes in me. Catherine Preziosi and Tom Hall are friends who were there when I started and there when I finished, and never stopped believing that my writing process would be successful.

For those who helped make the book better, I'll name Whitney Quesenbery (who told me to tear it up and start over), Peter Morville (who pointed out the good things about that first draft), and Kristina Podnar (who was generous with her knowledge and had good answers to countless queries that started out "Does this make sense to you?") Also, thanks to every client and colleague whom I've worked with for the last 15 years. You've taught me the most.

For those who poked and prodded me to the finish line, I'll name every conference attendee and tweeter who asked, "When's the book going to be done?" Shame can take you a long way. Also, I want to thank Simon Lande whose persistent but nice queries helped me run the last mile.

Lastly, I want to make a special category for my editor, Marta Justak, whose expertise is reflected on every page. Marta helped me to sound more like myself, pushed me to make things simpler and clearer, and offered me more than a few therapy sessions over the phone.

To all of you, I'm very grateful.

ABOUT THE AUTHOR

In a 20-year career, **Lisa Welchman** has paved the way in the discipline of digital governance, helping organizations stabilize their complex, multistakeholder digital operations. Lisa's focus centers on understanding and interpreting how the advent and prolific growth of digital impacts organizations, as well as the maturation of digital as a distinct vocational discipline in the enterprise.

Lisa began her career in digital in Silicon Valley in 1995 coding Web pages for Netscape, and was a program manager for Web publishing at Cisco Systems before establishing WelchmanPierpoint, a consultancy focused on large website management, in 1999. At WelchmanPierpoint, Lisa conducted early governance projects and established the first structured methodology for assessing digital governance maturity for clients including governmental agencies, NGOs, higher education institutions, and large multinational businesses. WelchmanPierpoint was acquired by ActiveStandards in 2014. Currently, Lisa speaks globally on issues related to digital governance, the rise of the Information Age, and the role of the information worker.